# GUIDE TO THE
# *Gardens*
## OF
# *Florida*

## LILLY PINKAS
### PHOTOGRAPHS BY JOSEPH PINKAS
Line illustrations by Frank Lohan

PINEAPPLE PRESS, INC.
SARASOTA, FLORIDA

Inquiries should be addressed to:
Pineapple Press, Inc.
P.O. Box 3899
Sarasota, Florida 34230

Library of Congress Cataloging-in-Publication Data

Pinkas, Lilly.
    Guide to the gardens of Florida / by Lilly Pinkas ; photographs by
Joseph Pinkas.—1st ed.
        p.      cm.
Includes index.
ISBN 1-56164-169-3 (alk. paper)
1. Gardens—Florida—Guidebooks. 2. Florida—Guidebooks.
I. Title.
SB466.U65F67  1998
712'.09759—dc21                                98-30009
                                               CIP


First Edition
10 9 8 7 6 5 4 3 2 1

Design by Osprey Design Systems, Bradenton, Florida
Typesetting by Sandra Wright's Designs, Sanford, Florida
Printed by BookCrafters, Chelsea, Michigan

# Acknowledgments

I would like to express my sincere thanks to Don Evans, Director of Horticulture at the Fairchild Tropical Garden, Miami, for his availability and patience at all times in answering the questions I have had. A very special thanks goes to Dr. Brinsley Burbidge, Director of the Fairchild Tropical Garden, for his precious time and advice in reviewing the manuscript. Many thanks also go to Mary Collins, Horticulturist at the Fairchild Tropical Garden, for her help with plant identification.

And, the biggest thanks goes to Lenka Wagner, for editing the first drafts of the manuscript, a truly Herculean task to say the least.

Northwest

Tallahassee

Point Washington

Jacksonville

Gainesville

St. Augustine

Palatka

Northeast

Central

Palm Coast

Maitland

Central East

Orlando

Kissimmee

Ormond Brach

Central West

Port Orange

Tampa

Winter Haven

Melbourne

St. Petersburg

Lake Wales

Vero Beach

Fort Pierce

Sarasota

Osprey

West Palm Beach

Palm Beach

Southeast

North Fort Myers

Coconut
Creek

Delray Beach

Fort Myers

Davie

Fort Lauderdale

North Miami Beach

Naples

Miami
Coral Gables
Coconut Grove
Homestead

Florida

Southwest

Key West

The Keys

# *Table of Contents*

*continues*

# Foreword

Florida is a state that, even in the sound of its name, conjures up visions of palm-fringed beaches and lush tropical vegetation— a land where nature is firmly in control and gardening is a heroic effort to control and give some semblance of order to plants that grow twelve months a year. It often feels like this to the Florida gardener. However, Florida offers more than subtropical weather where frosts are a rarity. It is a state with a wide range of climates and soil types, lies further north than New Orleans, and heads south to the archipelago of the Florida Keys, which penetrates climate-zone 11, where frosts are unknown. It is a state that is called home by gardeners who have brought gardening styles from many parts of the world, allowing them to flourish with a local bias. Hurricanes add just a hint of impermanence, but what garden ever remained static?

This book celebrates the diversity of Florida gardens and is a practical visitors' guide with neighboring gardens appearing close together in the text. If you have enjoyed one garden, there are often two or three within reach that will enhance your experience. It is also a guide compiled, not from brochures, but from the first-hand experiences and photography of Joe and Lilly Pinkas, who combine a deep aesthetic appreciation of gardens and garden design with personal gardening experience. As volunteers at Fairchild Tropical Garden, they know gardens and have an insider's knowledge of what it takes to make a great garden. They have used their backgrounds to provide a personal garden tour of this wonderful state, starting in the north and ending in the Florida Keys. If they give a garden their seal of approval, it is a gardener's garden; if you are a gardener, you will love it also.

No gardener will ever tell you that you are visiting a garden at the best time. Whenever you show up it is always, "you should have been here last week when the azaleas were in flower," or "come back next week when our jade vine will be at its best," or "be here in summer when everything looks green." This book attempts to suggest what could be the best times to visit. Follow their advice if you can, but never postpone a visit because you might be too early or too late for the garden's signature flowering. In truth, anytime is a good time to visit a garden. There is always something to see, and Florida has a longer season than most.

This book is both a great read and an enticing photographic account of what Florida has in store for you. It is a gourmet guide to the best of Florida gardens written and photographed by excellent gardeners who love to view others' gardens as well as cultivate their own. They are the best of guides. Follow them and you will love our state on a whole new level—Florida, the gardening state.

Dr. Brinsley Burbidge
Director, Fairchild Tropical Garden

# Introduction

The sixty gardens described in this book are certainly a varied group. They range in size from a half acre to four hundred acres. While many of them are "true" botanical gardens, others are primarily commercial enterprises. Their origins are as diverse as their present resources or specific goals. But regardless of whether their main purpose is to display, research, educate, conserve, or just simply amuse, in their own special way their common denominator is being places of beauty and harmony in the ever-changing environment. They are oases of quiet peace in our increasingly complex, noisy, and hurried world.

We wanted our list of gardens to be as comprehensive as possible. We crisscrossed the state in search of gardens, and we believe we did not miss any. (But if you find one we missed, please write to us in care of the publisher so we can include it in the next edition.) The sixty additional places mentioned are not gardens per se, but could be of interest to garden and plant lovers.

While visiting the gardens and traveling throughout Florida, it seemed logical to start at the northern part of the state and end in the south. That is why the gardens are presented in this order. The first garden described is Maclay State Gardens in Tallahassee, and the last one is the West Martello Tower in Key West. You can't go more south than that in Florida.

On our trips we experienced the entire spectrum of Florida's climate. Cool winters in northern Florida, where frost is the norm, through the temperate climate of central Florida, to south Florida, with semitropical conditions essentially year-round. We felt that including the proper travel directions certainly makes the trips easier and more enjoyable, and the complete address and phone number for each garden should make it easier for you to inquire before you go concerning best times to visit, flowering peaks, and any changes in the garden's hours, facilities, etc.

We sincerely hope that as you visit the gardens you will have as much fun and see as much beauty as we did.

# Northwest

Northwest    ● Tallahassee

Point Washington ●

# Maclay State Gardens

*A 28 acre garden where native plants are used extensively in landscaping. Over 150 varieties of camellias and 50 varieties of azaleas are represented.*

**Address:** 3540 Thomasville Road, Tallahassee, FL 32308
**Directions:** From I-10 take exit 30 (U.S. 319) and go north about 3 miles. The gardens will be on your left.
**Hours:** Open daily 8:00 a.m. to sunset
**Admission fee:** yes
**Wheelchair access:** partial
**Facilities:** none
**Available:** Guided tours are conducted Saturday and Sunday during the peak bloom around mid-March. Special tours may be arranged with three weeks advance notice.
**Area:** 28 acres
**Phone:** (850) 487-4556

Just a few miles from the Florida state capital of Tallahassee, tucked away in the rolling hills overlooking Lake Hall, are the Maclay State Gardens. Initially the property served as the southern retreat of New York financier Alfred B. Maclay and his family. In 1923 he decided to develop the gardens and in the process created a masterpiece of floral architecture. After his death in 1944, Mrs. Maclay continued the development according to his plans. Mrs. Maclay donated the gardens to the state of Florida in 1953.

As one approaches the gardens, the **pines** and **mixed hardwoods** so typical of this area are readily apparent. Once inside, massive **oaks** and huge pines tower over smaller understory specimens. The garden seems to be composed of several smaller gardens, every turn of the walkway revealing something new or unexpected to admire. Native plants are used extensively in landscaping, but there are also more than 160 exotic species or varieties adding diversity in shape, texture and color. Over 150 varieties of **camellias** and 50 varieties of **azaleas** are the predominant flowering shrubs throughout the gardens.

As one walks the house walk from the entry gate to the house, especially during the spring months, the unbelievable color experience begins to dazzle: a profusion of azalea blossoms, **southern magnolia** (*Magnolia grandiflora*), **saucer magnolia** (*Magnolia x soulangiana*) blossoms, white blossoms of the **dogwood tree** (*Cornus florida*), purplish/pink blossoms of the **redbud tree** (*Cercis canadensis*) and in late spring the blossoms of the beautiful native **mountain laurel** (*Kalmia latifolia*). Blossoms, blossoms everywhere!

The camellia walk, connecting the house and the walled garden, certainly showcases the beauty of thousands upon thousands of camellia blossoms with a color spectrum ranging from snowy white, through pink, to the deepest of reds. At the beginning of the camellia walk stands the first camellia planted in the gardens in 1923. At that time, when it was moved into the garden from another location, it was already said to be eighty to one hundred years old. Brick walls covered with climbing fig enclose the walled garden with its central fountain and white and blue della Robbia plaque on the west wall. A look through the gate on the east wall provides a gorgeous view of a long reflecting pool bordered by azaleas and tall palms with Lake Hall in the distance. Just outside the walled garden the magnificent pink blossoms of the native but now endangered **Chapman's rhododendron** *(Rhododendron chapmanii)* quietly contrast with the brick wall.

When you take the pine needle path from the walled garden to the pond, you will be surrounded by walls of camellias and gardenias growing under the tall **viburnum trees** (*Viburnum macrocephalum*) and **tea olive** (*Osmanthus fragrans*). The dark red, starlike flowers of **Florida anise** (*Illicium floridanum*) add still another dimension to the color spectrum.

The pond itself was built to reflect the colors of the surrounding plantings in its calm water. It certainly does that and more. This area is peaceful and serene. The tall evergreens to the south of the pond form a solid backdrop for flowering trees; a multitude of irises and daylilies provide splashes of color closer to the ground. The azalea hillside and **Oriental magnolia** plantings gently rise from the bank of the pond under the canopy of native oaks and pines. This section is simply breathtaking.

Or maybe you want to find the Secret garden? It is really not that difficult to find and you will enjoy it when you find it.

The lakeside path will lead you to Lake Hall, a habitat for fish, turtles, alligators and migrating water birds. In this area one can see one of the few remaining stands of **Torreya trees** (*Torreya taxiflora*). This beautiful evergreen tree was completely decimated by fungal blight in many other areas. The native plant arboretum showcases the native plants for use in landscape design.

When is the best time to visit here? Hard to say. The gardens change from week to week; there are always new blossoms and colors to admire. Plan to return here; one visit may not be enough.

*Worth Seeing:* Maclay House is open January through April and is complete with original furnishings from the Maclay family.

# Goodwood Museum and Gardens

**Address:** 1600 Miccosukee Road, Tallahassee, FL 32308

**Directions:** From I-10 take exit 31A on U.S. 90 west (Tennessee Road) and go 6 1/2 miles. Travel north on Magnolia Drive (CR 265), and then turn right on Miccosukee Road.

**Hours:** 9:00 a.m. to 5:00 p.m. Monday through Friday

**Closed:** Saturday, Sunday, and major holidays

**Admission fee:** none

**Wheelchair access:** partial

**Facilities:** none

**Area:** 19 acres

**Phone:** (850) 877-4202

At the time of this writing, Goodwood Plantation mansion is being restored into a museum. The surrounding gardens have already undergone major restoration and work is still continuing. Upon entering you will see massive, majestic, moss-draped **live oaks**. Under their canopy are several smaller gardens to explore. During our spring visit the azaleas were magnificent. There is no question that when all the work is completed in 1999 the gardens are going to be a showplace.

# Brokaw-McDougall House

---

**Address:** 329 North Meridian Street, Tallahassee, FL 32301

**Directions:** From I-10 take exit 29 on Monroe Street, then travel east 3 blocks on Tennessee till Meridian. The house will be on your right.

**Hours:**  9:00 a.m. to 1:00 p.m. Monday to Friday

**Closed:** Saturday and Sunday, Easter, Thanksgiving and Christmas Day

**Admission fee:** none

**Wheelchair access:** partial

**Facilities:** none

**Area:**  2 acres

**Phone:** (850) 891-3900

This historic house from the 1850s is surrounded by formal gardens under the canopy of 200-year-old oaks. **Azaleas** and **camellias** provide extra color in the spring.

Listed in the National Register of Historic Places.

# Lemoyne Art Foundation

**Address:** 125 North Gadsden Street, Tallahassee, FL 32301

**Directions:** From I-10 take exit 29 south on Monroe Street to Park Avenue. Travel east for 2 blocks, then continue north on Gadsden Street for less than a block.

**Hours:** 10:00 a.m. to 5:00 p.m. Tuesday to Saturday, 1:00 p.m. to 5:00 p.m. Sunday

**Closed:** Monday, Easter, Thanksgiving, and Christmas day

**Admission fee:** donations

**Wheelchair access:** partial

**Area:** 1/2 acre

**Phone:** (850) 222-8800

Helen Lind Garden. Small but intimate sculpture garden with **boxwood**-lined brick paths, **camellias**, **azaleas** and **ferns**.

# Eden State Gardens

*Of all Florida's state gardens, Eden is smallest in size but not in beauty. In the spring the glory of azaleas and flowering trees in bloom is breathtaking.*

**Address:** P.O. Box 26, Point Washington, FL 32454
**Directions:** From I10 take exit 14 on Highway 331 and head south to Highway 98. Continue east on Highway 98 and follow the signs.
**Hours:** Open daily 8:00 a.m. to sundown
**Admission fee:** yes
**Wheelchair access:** yes
**Facilities:** none
**Area:** 10 1/2 acres
**Phone:** (850) 231-4214

Located in Florida's panhandle, not far from the small town of Point Washington on the banks of Tucker Bayou, is the smallest of Florida's state gardens. Yet it certainly is full of beauty, as well as rich in history.

Originally this was the home of lumberman William H. Wesley and his family. The Wesley mansion was occupied during the Civil War by Union troops and stayed in the family until the 1950s. In 1963 the property was purchased by Miss Lois Maxon, a *New York Times* writer who was instantly smitten by the mansion and its surrounding beauty. She decided to name it Eden and also make it resemble the famous garden of the same name. In addition

to refurbishing the mansion, she started to develop the grounds. In 1968 Miss Maxon donated Eden to the state of Florida in memory of her parents.

As you enter the gardens, your attention will be drawn to the majestic **live oak trees** (*Quercus virginiana*). Wrapped in moss, they quietly provide welcome shade. Two of the largest here are close to six hundred years old, and many others are between two hundred and four hundred years old.

Next you will notice the profusion of colors. In the spring, depending on the time of visit, you can admire the blossoms of thousands of **azaleas** or **camellias**. At the time of our visit, **redbud trees** (*Cercis canadensis*), leafless, but totally covered with pinkish/purple blossoms, and **dogwood trees** (*Cornus florida*), with a profusion of delicate white blossoms, were just magnificent.

This is a truly beautiful place to visit and enjoy. To quote Amos Bronson Alcott: "Who loves a garden still his Eden keeps. . . ." That seems quite appropriate here.

*Worth Seeing:* Wesley House is open for guided tours from 9:00 a.m. to 4:00 p.m. Thursday to Monday. A nominal fee is charged.

# Northeast

Jacksonville

Gainesville

St. Augustine

Palatka

*Northeast*

# Cummer Museum of Art and Gardens

*A small, intimate garden on the banks of the St. Johns River.*

**Address:** 829 Riverside Avenue, Jacksonville, FL 32204
**Directions:** From I-95 take the exit for downtown Jacksonville, (Riverside Avenue) and follow the signs.
**Hours:** 10:00 a.m. to 5:00 p.m. Wednesday, Friday and Saturday; Noon to 5:00 p.m. Sunday; 10:00 a.m. to dusk Tuesday and Thursday
**Closed:** Mondays and major holidays
**Admission fee:** yes
**Wheelchair access:** yes
**Facilities:** museum store
**Area:** 2 acres
**Phone:** (904) 356-6857

On the banks of the St. Johns River in downtown Jacksonville, Mr. and Mrs. Arthur Cummer built their home and planted their first garden in 1903. Later, they added more formal gardens, including the **English Garden** in 1910. During a visit to Italy, the Cummers fell in love with the gardens of Villa Gamberaia in Florence. They decided to recreate its traditional eighteenth-century design as their own **Italian Garden**, which was planted in 1931. Many changes and additions have been made in the gardens over the years, but the original design of Dr. H. Harold Hume was essentially kept intact.

Shortly after entering the gardens, the commotion and noise of the surrounding city seem to disappear, allowing you to enjoy the gardens without distraction. The upper level of the formal gardens is shaded by a tremendous **live oak tree** (*Quercus virginiana*) that spans more than 150 feet and is estimated to be 250 years old. During spring, azaleas that were introduced into the garden in late 1920s bloom in the **Azalea Garden**, while summer brings thousands of beautiful **lily of the Nile** (*Agapanthus africanus*) blossoms. The play of sunlight on the freestanding, ivy-covered brick wall prompts a quiet, contemplative moment. In the early morning mist, the brick path bordered by trimmed hedges seems to end at the St. Johns River, or perhaps it has no end at all. A true delight.

*Worth Seeing:* The art exhibits of the Cummer Museum of Art range from Medieval, Renaissance, seventeenth century, Baroque, eighteenth century, Rococo, Meissen, nineteenth century, and Impressionism to modern works of the twentieth century. Travelling exhibitions are presented as well.

# Oldest House

**Address:** 14 St. Francis Street, St. Augustine, FL 32084

**Directions:** From I-95 take exit 95 and go east on Rt. 16 until you reach U.S. 1. Make a right turn on U.S. 1 and continue until King Street. Make a left turn on King Street, which will lead into the historic district.

**Hours:** 9:00 a.m. to 5:00 p.m. daily

**Closed:** Christmas Day

**Admission fee:** yes

**Wheelchair access:** yes

**Facilities:** gift shop

**Area:** 1/2 acre

**Phone:** (904) 824-2872

St. Augustine's Oldest House (Gonzales-Alvarez House) is a locally famous historic house as well as a National Historic Landmark.

The ornamental gardens surrounding the house showcase plants typical of those grown by previous occupants. The displays and plantings fit their surroundings and are very pleasing. To make your visit even more informative and enjoyable, a map of the gardens and a detailed list of plants, flowers, trees and shrubs are available.

Don't forget to explore the rest of the historic downtown and the restored Spanish Quarter. You will be surprised how many small but interesting gardens you can find, sometimes in the most unlikely places.

# Ravine State Gardens

*With a 100-foot ravine and 40,000 azaleas flowering in the spring, what else is there to say but spectacular?*

**Address:** P.O. Box 1096, Palatka, FL 32178
**Directions:** From I-95 take exit 94 (SR 207) and go west until you reach Palatka. Follow the signs.
**Hours:** Open 8:00 a.m. to sundown daily
**Admission fee:** yes
**Wheelchair access:** partial
**Available:** guided tours
**Area:** 85 acres
**Phone:** (904) 329-3721

In the quiet town of Palatka, nestled on the west bank of the St. Johns River, are the Ravine State Gardens. Nature started these gardens; people completed them. The steep ravines were created by water flowing down the sandy ridges of the St. Johns western shore. With the passage of time, grasses, shrubs and trees were established, eventually developing into the mixed hardwood forest we see today.

In the 1930s, in the depths of the Depression, a Palatka contractor named Thomas Gillespie had the great idea to develop beautiful, terraced gardens to create jobs right away and to attract tourists for future generations. Initially he was ridiculed, but in 1933 the city of Palatka convinced the Federal Works Relief Administration to provide funding for the project. In November 1934, Gillespie's Ravine Gardens formally opened. The gardens were maintained by the city of Palatka until 1970, when they became part of the Florida state park system.

Near their entrance, the formal gardens display various flowering plants among brick paths and stone pillars. More than 40,000 **azaleas** were originally planted here, and azaleas still dominate the gardens. Their colors during the spring bloom are breathtaking, and when blossoming **camellias** join the show, the result is spectacular.

The ravines themselves drop well over 100 feet to calm, spring-fed reflecting ponds. These ponds are dotted with **water lilies** and provide a quiet, restful place to sit. Suspension bridges that cross the ravines high overhead are part of the six-mile network of walking trails. The gardens may also be viewed from a 1.8-mile loop road. However you plan to proceed, save enough time to explore it all.

# *Kanapaha Botanical Gardens*

*A sixty-two-acre botanical garden with many exciting collections and displays. Their Bamboo Garden holds the largest public collection of bamboo species in Florida.*

**Address:** 4625 Southwest 63rd Boulevard, Gainesville, FL 32608
**Directions:** From I-75 take exit 75 to Archer Road (SR 24) and go west about 1 mile. Watch for signs on your right.
**Hours:** 9:00 a.m. to 5:00 p.m. Monday, Tuesday and Friday; 9:00 a.m. to dusk Wednesday, Saturday and Sunday
**Closed:** Thursdays, Thanksgiving, Christmas Day
**Admission fee:** yes
**Wheelchair access:** yes
**Facilities:** gift shop
**Area:** 62 acres
**Phone:** (352) 372-4981

Located just outside of Gainesville, the Kanapaha Gardens received their name from nearby Lake Kanapaha. (The word "Kanapaha" originated from the Timuqua Indian phrase meaning "palmetto-roofed home.") The entrance road to the gardens, once an old Indian game trail, was also used by naturalist William Bartram during his explorations at the time of the American Revolution.

Kanapaha Botanical Gardens were established in 1978, when plantings were started. First opened to the public in 1986, the gardens are operated and maintained by the North Florida Botanical Society, a nonprofit, private educational organization.

The stately **oaks**, **large pines** and **magnolias** lend the gardens a feeling of openness, while the man-made displays and plantings blend into the natural landscape. Visitors are free to create their own walking tours, assisted by a detailed map that describes each display in this sixty-two-acre facility.

The **Azalea-Camellia Garden**, a recent addition, provides color to the gardens during late winter and early spring. Most of the plantings here are cultivars of **camellia** (*Camellia japonica*) and various hybrids and cultivars of **azaleas** (*Rhododendron spp.*).

The **Bamboo Garden** holds the largest public collection of bamboo species in Florida. Bamboos are grasses, some with woody stems, and are one of the fastest growing plants in the world. When their shoots start to emerge, they grow several inches in a single day. Locally we cultivate bamboo for its ornamental qualities, but in other parts of the world, bamboo is highly valued as a building material. **Arrow bamboo** (*Pseudosasa japonica*), **giant bamboo** (*Dendrocalamus giganteus*), **black bamboo** (*Phyllostachys nigra*), **fern-leaf bamboo** (*Bambusa multiplex*) and **giant timber bamboo** (*Phyllostachys bambusoides*) are just a few species on display in the Bamboo Garden.

The **Palm Hammock** contains the most extensive display of cold-resistant palm species in north Florida. Some unusual double-crowned and even one triple-crowned **cabbage palms** (*Sabal palmetto*) can be seen here.

The **Sunken Garden** was created in a large sinkhole. Here the cool shade of **shumard oaks** (*Quercus shumardii*) and **box elder trees** (*Acer negundo*) provide the moist microclimate preferred by many plants. Several species of **ferns** and **gingers** also thrive in this area.

The **Bog Garden,** with the **water-lily** pond as its centerpiece, shows its beauty to the fullest during the warm summer months. The best time of day here is late morning, close to midday, when both day-flowering and night-flowering species are open at the same time. The **Brazilian Victoria water lily** (*Victoria amazonica*), the world's largest water lily, flowers here during the late summer and early fall.

The **Herb Garden,** one of the largest in Florida, consists of the medicinal garden, the scented garden and the knot garden, where geometric herb plantings display contrasts in texture or color.

The **Vinery** features a large collection of ornamental flowering vines. Also worthy of exploration are the **Crinum Garden,** the **Perennial Garden,** the **Cycad Garden,** the **Fern Cobble,** the **Rock Garden,** the **Hummingbird Garden,** the **Butterfly Garden,** the **Woodland Wildflower Garden,** the **Carnivorous Plant Garden** and the **Arboretum.**

In this part of Florida, the seasons are quite pronounced, and the corresponding changes in the gardens certainly reflect that. The summer months offer the most color, but every season carries its own rewards.

# Central

Central

Maitland

Orlando
Kissimmee

Winter Haven

Lake Wales

# Maitland Art Center

**Address:** 231 West Packwood Avenue, Maitland, FL 32751

**Directions:** From I-4 take exit 47 on Maitland Boulevard (SR 414) and go east. Make a right turn and go south on U.S. 17-92 until you reach Packwood Avenue, then go 3 blocks west off U.S. 17-92 on Packwood Avenue.

**Hours:** 10:00 a.m. to 4:30 p.m. Monday through Friday; Noon to 4:30 p.m. Saturday and Sunday

**Closed:** major holidays

**Admission fee:** donation

**Wheelchair access:** yes

**Facilities:** museum store

**Available:** membership

**Area:** 3 acres

**Phone:** (407) 539-2181

Located just minutes from Orlando, the Maitland Art Center's tranquil atmosphere presents a real contrast to the city streets. It began in the early 1930s as a winter retreat for its founder, artist/architect Andre Smith, and eventually evolved into an artists' colony with twenty-two buildings. Smith designed the unique stucco buildings as well as their courtyards and gardens using bas reliefs, murals and carvings done in an Aztec/Maya style. The Maitland Art Center includes a main garden with a reflecting pond and several smaller gardens. As you stroll along the paths, new courtyards and small gardens appear, one after every turn. This serene and peaceful place is listed as a State of Florida Historic Site and has earned a spot on the National Register of Historic Places.

# University of Central Florida Arboretum

*This arboretum located on the campus of the University of Central Florida combines more than 600 species of native plants and exotics.*

**Address:** 4000 Central Florida Boulevard, Orlando, FL 32816

**Directions:** From I-95 take Colonial Boulevard (Rt. 50) and go west. Make a right turn to Alafaya Trail (Rt. 434) and go north. The entrance to the campus will be on your right; the arboretum is located right on campus.

**Hours:** 9:00 a.m. to 4:00 p.m. daily

**Admission fee:** no

**Wheelchair access:** yes

**Area:** 80 acres

**Phone:** (407) 823-2141

Just outside of busy Orlando, almost hidden on a sprawling campus, is the University of Central Florida Arboretum. Many inviting trails and walkways allow you to explore the quiet arboretum; most likely you will have the entire place for yourself. Adding colorful blossoms to this setting are many **azaleas** and **magnolias**.

The exhibits and specimens are meticulously labeled with not only common and Latin names, but quite often with an additional short description or explanation. (Some of the native and exotic plants were introduced for various biology courses.) In all, more than 600 species have been reported in the Arboretum.

The main areas include:

**Native Plant Area,** with nice specimens of **sweetgum** (*Liquidambar styraciflua*), **Florida yew** (*Taxus floridiana*), **basswood** (Tilia americana), **needle palm** (*Rhapidophyllum hystrix*) and **cinnamon fern** (*Osmunda cinnamomea*), **palmetto palm** (*Sabal palmetto*) and **longleaf pine** (*Pinus palustris*) communities.

Five-acre **Cypress Dome,** with the older and taller trees in its

center and younger trees on the periphery. It is not common to
see a stand of cypress in central Florida.

**Stockard Conservatory** houses cold-sensitive plants, mainly
**orchids, bromeliads,** bananas and pineapples.

**Live Oak Hammock,** with not only **live oak** *(Quercus virginiana)*
but also nice specimens of **Chapman's oak** *(Quercus Chapmanii)*
and **shumard oak** *(Quercus shumardii).*

# Harry P. Leu Gardens

*A fifty-acre botanical garden with many outstanding collections, including the largest camellia collection in eastern North America and the largest formal rose garden in Florida.*

**Address:** 1920 North Forest Avenue, Orlando, FL 32803
**Directions:** From I-4 take exit 43 on Princeton Street and continue until Princeton Street dead ends at Mills Street (Hwy 17-92). Make a right turn and continue on Mills Street to the second traffic light, then make a left turn on Virginia Drive. Continue on Virginia Drive for about 1 mile, bear left, follow the signs; the gardens will be on your left.
**Hours:** 9:00 a.m. to 5:00 p.m. daily
**Closed:** Christmas Day
**Admission fee:** yes
**Wheelchair access:** yes
**Facilities:** gift shop, library
**Available:** membership, classes, lectures, guided garden tours
**Area:** 49 acres
**Phone:** (407) 246-2620

Within the city of Orlando on the shores of Lake Rowena, the majestic trees and fine plant collections of the Harry P. Leu Gardens provide a quiet refuge from the bustle of this vibrant city.

Harry P. Leu was a prominent businessman who took immense pride and enjoyment in developing his estate into a local showplace. In addition to **oaks**, **camellias** and **azaleas**, the gardens contain many exotic plants that Mr. Leu and his wife collected during their worldwide travels. On January 1, 1961, the couple officially presented their home and gardens as a gift to the city of Orlando.

The gardens' future is reflected in its mission statement: "Harry P. Leu Gardens seeks to become an exemplary garden of historical significance. To further its mission, Harry P. Leu Gardens will: educate through the creation and maintenance of plant collections and through the gathering and dissemination of horticultural information; foster the enjoyment of the beauty of plants through a variety of displays and activities in a preserved natural setting."

The gardens offer a variety of distinct sections as well as special collections. In the **North and South Woods**, the **live oak** (*Quercus virginiana*), **laurel oak** (*Quercus laurifolia*), **longleaf pine** (*Pinus palustris*), **sweet gum** (*Liquidambar styraciflua*) and a few species of palms provide a dense, high canopy for an understory of beautiful camellias. The 2,000 specimens of the famous **Camellia Collection** represent the largest gathering of camellias in eastern North America. The collection contains more than 500 cultivars of *Camellia sasangua* and *Camellia japonica*. The **Ravine Garden** simulates the tropics with several plantings of **palms, ferns, gingers, aroids, bromeliads** and **bananas**. **White butterfly ginger** (*Hedychium coronarium*) and **scarlet ginger** (*Hedychium coccineum*) add color to the rest of the gardens. In the **Xerophyte Garden** the arid, rocky landscape serves as a background to several **cactus** and **agave** species. The controlled environment of the **Display Greenhouse** nurtures **orchids, bromeliads, ferns** and **anthuriums**.

The **Rose Garden**, with its central fountain surrounded by four corner gazebos, showcases more than 1,500 roses of nearly 250 varieties, including grandiflora, floribunda, hybrid tea, shrub and climber. It is the largest formal rose garden in Florida. In the **White Garden** several species show off white blossoms or variegated foliage. The **Palm Garden** displays cycads as well as one of the most extensive collections of palms in Central Florida. More than 100 types of palms are being researched here for their cold-resistance. Several cultivars of **bamboo** can be found nearby.

**Wyckoff Overlook** includes a gazebo and boardwalk with a view of Lake Rowena. Planted with native wetland plants, the overlook is an ideal spot to observe birds and wildlife and to admire the beautiful specimens of **bald cypress** (*Taxodium distichum*) and **pond cypress** (*Taxodium ascendens*) that rise along the lakeshore.

Don't miss the **Daylily Collection**, with over 100 species and cultivars of Hemerocallis, the **Hibiscus Collection**, the **Native Plant Garden,** the **Butterfly Garden**, or the **Herb Garden**. Without a doubt, the **Floral Clock** will also catch your attention.

*Worth Seeing:* The Leu House Museum, illustrating turn-of-the-century Florida living. This restored nineteenth-century farmhouse is listed in the National Register of Historic Places. Guided tours given on the hour and half-hour. Hours: 10:00 a.m. to 4:00 p.m. Tuesday through Saturday; 1:00 p.m. to 4:00 p.m. Sunday and Monday.

The Garden House, a 22,000-square-foot education center, houses an exhibit hall, museum and theater. The library and garden shop are located on the first floor.

# A World of Orchids

**Address:** 2501 Old Lake Wilson Road, Kissimmee, FL 34747
**Directions:** From I-4 take exit 25B, go 2 miles west on U.S. 192,
    then 1 mile south on Old Lake Wilson Road (CR 545).
**Hours:** 9:30 a.m. to 5:30 p.m. daily
**Closed:** New Year's Day, Fourth of July, Thanksgiving, Christmas
    Day
**Admission fee:** yes
**Wheelchair access:** yes
**Facilities:** gift shop
**Available:** guided tours, group rates, membership, school programs,
    free orchid classes
**Area:** 10 acres, 1/2-acre conservatory
**Phone:** (407) 396-1887

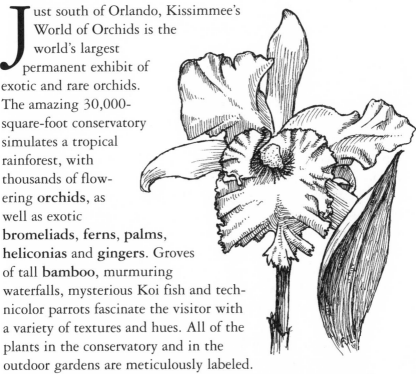

Just south of Orlando, Kissimmee's World of Orchids is the world's largest permanent exhibit of exotic and rare orchids. The amazing 30,000-square-foot conservatory simulates a tropical rainforest, with thousands of flowering **orchids**, as well as exotic **bromeliads, ferns, palms, heliconias** and **gingers**. Groves of tall **bamboo,** murmuring waterfalls, mysterious Koi fish and technicolor parrots fascinate the visitor with a variety of textures and hues. All of the plants in the conservatory and in the outdoor gardens are meticulously labeled.

A World of Orchids also offers a **rose** gazebo and a boardwalk.

# Cypress Gardens

*The Botanical Gardens in Cypress Gardens are truly beautiful, featuring fascinating displays and more than 8,000 varieties of plants.*

**Address:** P.O. Box 1, Cypress Gardens, FL 33884 (near Winter Haven)
**Directions:** From I-4 exit 23, take U.S. 27 south until you reach SR 540. Continue west on SR 540 (Cypress Gardens Boulevard) for 4 miles and follow the signs. (The gardens are impossible to miss.)
**Hours:** 9:30 a.m. to 5:30 p.m. daily
**Admission fee:** yes
**Wheelchair access:** yes
**Facilities:** several shops, boutiques, and restaurants
**Available:** special group rates
**Area:** 223 acres
**Phone:** (941) 324-2111, (800) 282-2123

L ocated in Central Florida, just about halfway between Orlando and Tampa, the beautiful Cypress Gardens will amuse and educate you in many different ways.

After purchasing sixteen acres along the shores of Lake Eloise in the early 1930s, the Pope family set out to transform a reclaimed cypress swampland into a botanical garden. After opening to the public in 1936, the gardens grew in size and in popularity. Many additional attractions were added over the years, the famous water-skiing show being one of the original attractions. Presently Cypress Gardens occupies more than 200 acres and is without question an internationally recognized theme park.

Aside from the attractions and amusements, the Botanical Gardens are certainly not to be missed. Cypress Gardens features more than 8,000 varieties of plants (tropical, subtropical and temperate). Following the meandering walkways allows the visitor to wonder in amazement at the surrounding displays. Majestic **live oaks** (*Quercus virginiana*) and **bald cypress** (*Taxodium distichum*) provide welcome shade. The trails will also lead you through the **Tea and Spice Garden**, the **Oriental Garden**, the **Rose Garden**, the

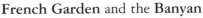

**French Garden** and the **Banyan Terrace**, just to mention a few. The displays are meticulously maintained and very well marked, with signs indicating both common and Latin names as well as the country of origin.

If you still want to see more flowers and plants, then explore **Plantation Gardens** or **Butterfly Conservatory**. The recently opened **Biblical Garden** features plants named in the Bible. Cypress Gardens also celebrates nature with four flower festivals every year: the Spring Flower Festival, the Victorian Garden Party, the Mum (Chrysanthemum) Festival and the Poinsettia Festival.

Better save an entire day for Cypress Gardens.

*Worth Seeing:* Birds of Prey, Reptile Discovery, Birdwalk Aviary, Animal Habitats, Water Ski shows, Ice Skating shows, and the list just goes on. **Birds of Prey** program includes falcons, owls and a turkey vulture. **Reptile Discovery** show features alligators, crocodiles, an albino python, an alligator turtle, a rat, corn snakes and iguanas. **Birdwalk Aviary** is a 3,000-square-foot free-flight aviary. **Animal Habitats** features alligators, capybaras and wallabies.

# Slocum Water Gardens

**Address:** 1101 Cypress Gardens Boulevard, Winter Haven, FL 33884

**Directions:** From I-4 take U.S. 27 south until you reach SR 540 (Cypress Gardens Boulevard), continue west for 5 1/2 miles, and the gardens will be on your left.

**Hours:** 8:00 a.m. to 5:00 p.m. Monday through Friday, 8:00 a.m. to noon Saturday

**Closed:** Sundays and major holidays

**Admission fee:** no

**Wheelchair access:** yes

**Area:** 1 acre

**Phone:** (941) 293-7151

Since 1938, the Slocum Water Gardens has specialized in the cultivation of **water lilies**. Many varieties of lilies are showcased here, in a wide range of colors and sizes, with tropical varieties blooming day and night. If aquatic gardening interests you, don't miss this place. In addition to water lilies, other aquatic plants, fish, water gardening hardware and valuable advice is available here.

# Bok Tower Gardens

*One hundred and thirty acres surround the Singing Tower on top of the Florida peninsula's highest point: Iron Mountain.*

**Address:** 1151 Tower Boulevard, Lake Wales, FL 33853

**Directions:** From I-95 take SR 60 west to Rt. 17B. Go 2 miles and make a left turn on Rt. 17A (Burns Avenue). Continue on Burns Avenue until you see the sign for the Bok Tower Gardens on your right.

**Hours:** 8:00 a.m. to 6:00 p.m. daily

**Admission fee:** yes

**Wheelchair access:** yes

**Facilities:** gift shop, restaurant, education and visitors' center

**Available:** membership, guided tours, lectures, workshops

**Area:** 130 acres

**Phone:** (941) 676-1408; recorded information (941) 676-9412

The Bok Tower Gardens are nestled on top of the sandy hill that some still refer to as Iron Mountain. At 298 feet above sea level, this is the highest elevation in Florida.

The gardens resulted from the dreams of Edward Bok, a remarkably successful, Dutch-born author and magazine editor. While spending his winters in this area, Bok greatly enjoyed walks among the pines and scrub palmettos of Iron Mountain and watching sunsets from the mountain's top. He was inspired to preserve this special place as an oasis of peace and serenity that would touch the soul with its quiet beauty.

Bok visualized a refuge for wildlife as well as for people. In the center of the gardens, he would build a beautiful tower to house a carillon. The glorious pure sound of the carillon bells would enhance the quiet beauty of the sanctuary gardens.

In 1923, Bok retained the famous landscape architect Frederick Law Olmstead to design the grounds and gardens, and the architect Milton B. Medary to design the tower. In 1929, the completed gardens and tower were dedicated on behalf of Edward Bok by President Calvin Coolidge as a gift to the American people. Mr. Bok's dream of combining the beauty of wildlife, plant life and the music for the enjoyment of future visitors was realized.

The following quotations best describe the visitor's experience at the Bok Tower Gardens. In 1956, the renowned landscape architect William Lyman Phillips wrote: "The gardens, once entered, affect the senses of the visitor gratefully, create a poetic mood, induce feelings of reverence, stir the mind to rapt admiration. Here voices are hushed as in a church and decency for the moment takes possession of the vulgar . . . A more striking example of the power of beauty could hardly be found, better proof that here beauty exists could not be asked for." And John Burroughs most eloquently summarized his feelings about his visits by writing: "I come here to find myself. It is so easy to get lost in the world."

The Bok Tower Gardens now cover about 130 acres, of which about half is semi-wild. Just past the entrance and the bronze dedication plaque, there are several interesting evergreens: **yew podocarpus** (*Podocarpus macrophyllus*), **broad-leaf podocarpus** (*Podocarpus nagi*) as well as large, fragrant specimens of the **camphor tree** (*Cinnamomum camphora*).

Near the Reflecting Pool that surrounds the Singing Tower grows an array of mostly native Florida palms. The **cabbage palms** (*Sabal palmetto*), the state tree of Florida, were planted by President and Mrs. Coolidge at the dedication ceremony in 1929. Endangered **needle palms** (*Rhapidophyllum hystrix*) and **everglades palms** (*Acoelorrhaphe wrightii*) can be seen in this area as well as **lady palms** (*Rhapis excelsa*).

Stately **oak trees** (*Quercus virginiana*) spread their canopies above the **Live Oak Grove** south of the Singing Tower, with **Spanish moss** (*Tillandsia usneoides*) hanging from their branches. This is a very peaceful section of the garden that overlooks Lake Wales and the surrounding citrus groves.

**Pine Ridge Trail** leads to the **Pine Ridge Nature Preserve,** where natural conditions are preserved without any outside disturbances whatsoever. No fallen trees are removed, no dead trees are cut; everything is left up to nature to dispose of in its own way.

Many other walkways, such as **North Walk, Mockingbird Walk, Overlook Walk,** and **Sword Fern Path** lead you through various sections of the garden. The walks feature a pleasing combination of native and exotic plants. The green canopies of **pines, oaks** and **palms** frame the magnificent blossoms of **azaleas, magnolias, camellias** and **gardenias.**

From **Window by the Pond,** a nature observatory, visitors can view the wildlife of a freshwater pond with minimal disturbance to creatures living in this area. Indeed, Bok Tower Gardens has been playing an important role in natural preservation. Since 1986 the Endangered Plant Program here has focused on the conservation of Florida's rarest native plants.

This garden, designated a National Historic Landmark in 1993, certainly is a special place.

*Worth Seeing:* The **Singing Tower** is said to be the most beautiful bell tower in the world. Standing 205 feet tall, built of pink and gray Georgia marble and Florida coquina rock, the tower houses a 57-bell carillon. The carillon's largest bell weighs over eleven tons, while the smallest weighs only seventeen pounds. Since the Singing Tower opened in 1929, its bells have sounded every day. Carillon recitals are given daily.

# Central East

Palm Coast

*Central East*

Ormond Brach
Port Orange
Melbourne
Vero Beach
Fort Pierce

# Washington Oaks State Gardens

*The largest of the Florida State Gardens, Washington Oaks encompasses 400 acres that range from rugged coastal landscapes to exotic formal gardens.*

**Address:** 6400 N. Oceanshore Boulevard, Palm Coast, FL 32137
**Directions:** From I-95 take exit 91C (Palm Coast) and go east to Hwy. A1A. Continue north on A1A for about 6 miles.
**Hours:** 8:00 a.m. to sundown daily
**Admission fee:** yes
**Wheelchair access:** yes
**Facilities:** none
**Area:** 400 acres
**Phone:** (904) 446-6780

Extending from the Matanzas River to the Atlantic Ocean, Washington Oaks State Gardens is the largest of the Florida State Gardens at 400 acres. This area was once a part of the Bella Vista Plantation owned by Joseph Hernandez, a militia general who commanded troops in north Florida during the Second Seminole War. A land surveyor named George Washington—a relative of the first president—married into the Hernandez family in the mid 1800s. In 1936 the property was purchased by Mr. and Mrs. Owen D. Young. Mr. Young, who was chairman of the board of General Electric, enlarged the existing gardens and expanded its groves and plantings. After Mr. Young's death in 1964, the entire property was donated to the state of Florida by his wife. Their home has since been converted into an interpretive center.

You can start your exploration of the gardens among the coquina rocks and crashing surf of the expansive, sandy beach. At low tide, crabs, starfish, anemones and other sea creatures fill the tidal pools—natural aquariums that reward a patient exploration.

Further inland and just past the beach is the coastal scrub zone. The stunted vegetation growing among the sand dunes here is well adapted to the dry, harsh, almost desert-like soil and climatic conditions. The scrub then gives way to the coastal hammock with its majestic **live oaks** (*Quercus virginiana*), **hickory** (*Carya spp.*), **red cedar** (*Juniperus lucayana*) and **southern magnolia** (*Magnolia grandiflora*).

51

Still further inland are the tidal marshes of the Matanzas River, where wading and migrating birds can be observed. It's delightful to sit on the riverbank in the evening and watch the sun disappear over the marshes, accompanied by the music of the river, the birds and the wind.

Under a canopy of **pines** and **oaks**, the formal gardens display many exotic species alongside reflecting pools, footpaths and brick walkways. In the spring, **azaleas** and **camellias** will astound you with a profusion of colorful blossoms, while the **Rose Garden** will intoxicate you with its fragrance and color.

Washington Oaks is a beautiful and unique garden and certainly worth a visit.

*Worth Seeing:* Owen D. Young's home has been converted into an interpretive center featuring the natural and cultural history of this area. The interpretive center is open from 9:00 a.m. to 5:00 p.m. daily.

# *Ormond Memorial Art Museum and Gardens*

*These four-acre gardens surrounding the Ormond Art Museum feature winding paths, gazebos, waterfalls, quiet streams and footbridges.*

**Address:** 78 East Granada Boulevard, Ormond Beach, FL 32176

**Directions:** From I-95 take exit 87 (Route 92) and go east until you reach U.S. 1. Make a left turn onto U.S. 1 and go north until you reach Granada Boulevard; the Gardens will be on your right.

**Hours:** Sunrise to sunset daily; Museum: 10:00 a.m. to 4:00 p.m. Monday through Friday, 12 noon to 4:00 p.m. Saturday and Sunday

**Closed:** major holidays (museum only)

**Admission fee:** donation (museum only)

**Wheelchair access:** yes

**Available:** membership, lectures, workshops

**Area:** 4 acres

**Phone:** (904) 676-3347

Just north of Daytona Beach is the small but active and vibrant city of Ormond Beach. In the late 1940s, when it was just a quiet beach resort, Ormond Beach received a gift of fifty-six paintings from the painter Malcom Frasier, a frequent visitor to this area. The city needed to properly house and display the paintings, however, so a group of dedicated citizens, with a great deal of community support, set to remodeling and expanding a small, vacant frame building into a museum. On December 29, 1946, the Ormond Memorial Art Museum opened as Florida's first memorial commemorating World War II.

The hard work of clearing the dense jungle surrounding the structure opened enough space to create these four-acre gardens, which combine sunny open spaces, shady paths, a dense canopy, waterfalls, gazebos and pleasant bridges over small streams.

A beautiful **American elm tree** (*Ulmus americanum*)—uncommon in these parts—can be seen here. As you walk around, the **water lilies** add color and **white gingers** (*Hedychium coronarium*) add a nice fragrance, making the Ormond Beach Memorial Gardens a pleasing experience.

*Worth Seeing:* Changing exhibitions at Ormond Memorial Art Museum featuring exhibits of Florida artists.

# Sugar Mill Botanical Gardens

*Interesting collections highlight this twelve-acre botanical garden on the site of an old sugar plantation.*

**Address:** 950 Old Sugar Mill Road, Port Orange, FL 32119
**Directions:** From I-95 take exit 85 and go east on Route 421 for about 5 miles. Make a left turn on U.S. 1 and go north. Make a left turn on Herbert Street, go about 1 mile, then make a sharp right turn on Old Sugar Mill Road. The gardens will be on your left.
**Hours:** dawn to dusk, daily
**Admission fee:** donation
**Wheelchair access:** yes
**Facilities:** gift shop
**Available:** membership, map for self-guided tour, guided group tour by appointment
**Area:** 12 acres
**Phone:** (904) 767-1735

Not far from Daytona Beach, tucked away in a quiet area of Volusia County, are the Sugar Mill Botanical Gardens. The site was originally the Dunlawton Plantation, a sugar-producing estate of the early 1800s that was partially destroyed in the Second Seminole War in 1836. During the Civil War years, the plantation was used by Confederate soldiers for making salt. In 1973 it was placed on the National Register of Historic Places. In 1988 the Botanical Gardens of Volusia, Inc., a nonprofit organization, took over the Dunlawton Sugar Mill ruins in order to establish and maintain the Sugar Mill Botanical Gardens.

Various trails meander through the garden under the high canopy of huge, majestic **live oak trees** *(Quercus virginiana)* and **sycamore trees** (*Platanus occidentalis*) that provide welcome shade. Collections of **camellias** and **magnolias** provide a splash of color, and the **cape jasmine** (*Gardenia jasminoides*) and **sweet olive** (*Osmanthus fragrans*) add deliciously pleasing scents to the experience. The **Holly Collection**, the **ivies** alongside **Ivy Lane**, **lilies**, **gingers** and **irises** all offer quite a variety of blossoms to enjoy. The **Dent Smith Palmetum** was established in honor of a local palm lover who was instrumental in founding the International Palm Society.

The old machinery and implements surviving at the sugar mill ruins provide a fascinating glimpse into the history of sugar-making.

# Botanical Gardens at the Florida Institute of Technology

*Discover thirty-five acres of lush tropical vegetation, natural streams, and thousands of palms on the campus of the Florida Institute of Technology.*

**Address:** 150 West University Boulevard, Melbourne, FL 32901
**Directions:** From I-95 take exit 71 and go east on Route 192 for about 6 miles. Make a right turn on Babcock Street (Route 507) and go about 1/2 mile into the FIT parking lot on your right.
**Hours:** 8:00 a.m. to 6:00 p.m. daily
**Admission fee:** no
**Wheelchair access:** yes
**Area:** 35 acres
**Phone:** (407) 768-8000, ext. 8986

Located about three miles from the heart of Melbourne, on the campus of the Florida Institute of Technology, are the Botanical Gardens. In contrast to the busy campus, the Botanical Gardens are a natural, quiet and serene place where one can forget the hurry of the surrounding world.

Beautiful wooden walkways that blend well with the surroundings meander under the dense canopy, over several natural streams and past scattered benches that invite the visitor to sit down and contemplate. Other trails wind through the sections of the gardens that have been left in a mostly natural state. The sun filters through the canopy of **live oaks** and their branches covered with **Spanish moss** and other **tillandsias**, while **aroids** climb the trunks. There are **palms**, palms everywhere, more than 2,000 of them, as well as **bamboos**, **ferns**, **bromeliads** and **gingers**.

# McKee Botanical Garden

**Address:** 350 South U.S. 1, Vero Beach, FL 32962

**Directions:** From I-95 take exit 66 to Hwy. 68 (Orange Avenue), make a left turn on King's Hwy. (Hwy. 713) and go north until you are on U.S. 1. Go north on U.S. 1 into Vero Beach; after you cross Oslo Road the gardens will be on your right.

**Hours:** After October 1, 1998, the gardens are closed until the grand opening in the summer of 1999. The new hours have yet to be established.

**Admission fee:** yes

**Facilities:** gift shop, café

**Area:** 20 acres

**Phone:** (561) 794-0601

This garden, which is still undergoing intensive restoration, will reopen to the public in the summer of 1999. But what a story!

A wealthy citrus grower, Waldo Sexton, and a millionaire engineer, Arthur McKee, had the idea of creating jungle gardens that would be open to the public. Sexton and McGee, both of whom took a strong interest in plants and plant collecting, corresponded with the famous plant explorer, Dr. David Fairchild, and commissioned a renowned landscape architect, William Lyman Phillips, to design the garden.

The McKee Garden started out in the early 1930s with eighty acres of native tropical hammock along the Indian River. Phillips' infrastructure of trails, streams and ponds and extensive plantings helped to transform this acreage into one of Florida's most popular attractions.

During World War II, the gardens were closed to the public but used by the military for training soldiers in the rigors of jungle warfare. Although the gardens were reopened after the war, they went into a gradual decline and finally closed in 1976. More than sixty acres of land were sold to condominium developers, and the rest almost met a similar fate. Luckily, a drive started to save the surviving portion, which represents the historic core of the original gardens.

In 1993, the Indian River Land Trust was established to lead the efforts to raise the money needed for the restoration of the garden. Countless hours were spent by hundreds of volunteers in clearing the twenty years' worth of neglect and uncontrolled plant growth.

Judging by what has been accomplished so far, there is no doubt that beauty will again return to the garden, which is planned for a public reopening in the summer of 1999.

# Heathcote Botanical Gardens

*A small, three-and-a-half-acre botanical garden that is just like a breath of fresh air, offering a beautiful Japanese garden, and displays of palms and flowering trees.*

**Address:** 210 Savannah Road, Ft. Pierce, FL 34982

**Directions:** From I-95 or from the Florida Turnpike take the Route 70 exit and go east to U.S. 1. Make a right turn (south) on U.S. 1 and after about 1/2 mile make a left turn on Savannah Road.

**Hours:** 9:00 a.m. to 5:00 p.m. Tuesday through Saturday; 1:00 p.m. to 5:00 p.m. Sundays from November through April

**Closed:** Mondays and major holidays

**Admission fee:** yes

**Wheelchair access:** yes

**Facilities:** gift shop

**Available:** membership, classes, lectures, guided tours by appointment

**Area:** 3 1/2 acres

**Phone:** (561) 464-4672

Begun only recently, the Heathcote Botanical Gardens in Fort Pierce are beginning to make a name for themselves. The gardens are still growing and undergoing further development and improvement.

The present gardens were started by Jim and Molly Crimmins as a commercial nursery. Over the years many new trees were planted, and the property was continuously improved. The Crimminses also designed and built a small Japanese garden on the north side of the property. The Japanese garden became a rallying point for local citizens when urban development threatened to destroy it. Fortunately, the decision was made to save not just the Japanese garden but the entire site. In 1985, Heathcote Botanical Gardens, Inc. was established as a not-for-profit corporation. The corporation's role and its vision for the site are best reflected by its mission statement: "The Mission of Heathcote Botanical Gardens is to establish a botanical garden which will inspire and delight visitors with its collection of quality ornamentals and native plants in well-designed and maintained displays, to serve as a repository of horticultural and botanical knowledge for the education of the public and to be a center for cultural activities and events."

One can start enjoying the gardens by exploring the **Palm Walk**, where over 40 species of **palms** and **cycads** can be seen. Nice specimens of **Australian fan palm** (*Livistonia australis*), **red fan palm** (*Livistonia mariae*), **European fan palm** (*Chamaerops humilis*), **ribbon fan palm** (*Livistonia decipiens*), **Chinese fan palm** (*Livistonia chinensis*) and **taraw palm** (*Livistonia saribus*) thrive here.

Just past the Palm Walk begins the area of **Flowering Vines** and **Flowering Trees**, which include a nice specimen of **silk floss tree** (*Chorisia speciosa*). A **Native Plant Area** follows, with many trees, shrubs and flowers native to subtropical Florida; **bromeliads** and **gingers** surround the **Memorial Garden**.

In the **Japanese Garden**, the sound of a gentle waterfall complements the seemingly simple positioning of rocks, earth, water and plants that is the key to Japanese garden design. **Weeping yew trees** (*Podocarpus gracilior*) and the permanent **bonsai** exhibit also grace this site.

The **Herb Garden**, **Bulb Beds** and **Subtropical Shade House** complete the garden walk, which is further enhanced by scattered rest areas.

# Central West

Central West

Tampa

St. Petersburg

Sarasota
Osprey

# University of South Florida Botanical Garden

*This small botanical garden on the campus of the University of South Florida displays hardy palms, riparian and temperate forests, bromeliads, and carnivorous plants, just to mention a few.*

**Address:** 4202 East Fowler Avenue, Tampa, FL 33620

**Directions:** From I-275 take Fowler Avenue exit east to 30th Street and turn north. From 30th Street make a right turn onto Pine Drive. The Garden entrance is at the intersection of Pine and Oak drives. From I-75 take the exit heading west on Fowler Avenue and follow the same directions as mentioned above.

**Hours:** 9:00 a.m. to 5:00 p.m. Monday through Friday; 9:00 a.m. to 4:00 p.m. Saturday; Noon to 4:00 p.m. Sunday

**Closed:** major holidays

**Admission fee:** no

**Wheelchair access:** yes

**Facilities:** plant shop

**Available:** membership, workshops, lectures, guided tours by appointment

**Area:** 6 acres

**Phone:** (813) 974-2329

Located on the campus of the University of South Florida, this botanical garden serves as a research and teaching center for the school's Department of Biology. The garden is, however, also open to the public and actively encourages public support and participation. The mission of the University of South Florida Botanical Garden is: "To develop collections, displays, research programs and educational programs, representing and interpreting the diversity of the Earth's plant life for the academic community and the general public." Started in 1969, the garden is gradually being improved and its exhibits enlarged.

The garden can be explored at a leisurely pace by simply following the trails; a USF Botanical Garden Trail Map is available to help you navigate. The exhibits throughout are clearly marked:

red signs identify Florida native plants, while blue signs indicate nonnative plants.

In the **Riparian Forest** and **Temperate Forest,** at the south part of the garden, grow nice specimens of **swamp chestnut oak** (*Quercus michauxii*), **turkey oak** (*Quercus laevis*) and **ear tree** (*Enterolobium contortisiliquum*). This section also contains a **Fruit Orchard** and a **Flowering Tree Exhibit.** The **White Sand Scrub** area represents another important habitat of Florida.

The high canopy of the **Rain Forest** exhibit is provided by, among others, a **live oak** (*Quercus virginiana*), a **camphor tree** (*Cinnamomum camphora*), a **montezuma cypress** *(Taxodium mucronatum)* and a **hercules club tree** (*Zantoxylum clava*). In the understory there are many **aroids, bromeliads** and **heliconias,** as well as some beautiful **gingers: kahili ginger** (*Hedychium gardneranum*), **blue ginger** *(Dichorisandra thyrsiflora)* and **shell ginger** (*Alpinia mutica*), just to name a few.

The **Palm Exhibit,** featuring hardy palms, the **Butterfly Garden** and the **Herb Garden** with its labeled collection of culinary herbs, also wait to be explored. Beautiful specimens of the **bunya bunya tree** (*Araucaria bidwillii*) and an **ipe tree** (*Tabebuia avellanedae*) provide a shady canopy for the **Bromeliad Garden.**

One unusual exhibit is not often seen in other gardens: a **Carnivorous Plants Bog.** The bog contains plants that have evolved in nutrient-poor areas and therefore depend on animal prey, rather than nutrients from the soil, to survive. In this section, even the aquatic carnivorous plants, such as **bladder worts** (*Utricularia*) are represented. Four main groups of carnivorous plants are represented: The one known best, **the Venus flytrap** (*Dionaea muscipula*); **pitcher plants:** (*Sarracenia minor*), (*Sarracenia flava*), (*Sarracenia leucophylla*), (*Sarracenia x formosana*) and (*Sarracenia psittacina*); **Butterworts:** (*Pinguicula lutea*), (*Pinguicula caerulea*) and (*Pinguicula aguatha x gypsicola*); **Sundews:** (*Drosera adelae*), (*Drosera binata*), (*Drosera capensis*), (*Drosera capillaris*), (*Drosera filiformis filiformis*), (*Drosera Filiformis tracyi*) and *(Drosera spathulata)*.

You will enjoy exploring this garden.

# *Eureka Springs Garden*

**Address:** 6400 Eureka Springs Road, Tampa, FL 33620
**Directions:** From I-4 take exit 6C; stay in the right lane until you reach Eureka Springs Road, follow this road 1 mile and the garden will be on your left.
**Hours:** 8:00 a.m. to 6:00 p.m. daily
**Closed:** Christmas Day, Thanksgiving
**Admission fee:** no
**Wheelchair access:** yes
**Facilities:** small picnic area with tables and grills
**Area:** 38 acres
**Phone:** (813) 744-5536

Eureka Springs Garden, located within Eureka Springs Park, is a peaceful hideaway not far from busy Tampa. The garden includes several walkways and a boardwalk for exploration of a multitude of native as well as exotic plants. Under the canopy of tall **pines** and **cedars**, **azaleas** are beautiful in the spring. There are displays of **orchids, ferns, bromeliads, tillandsias** and **gingers** in the greenhouse and screened pavilion. Much of the park surrounding the garden has been left in its natural state. Several winding trails will lead you through the park,

allowing you to observe many native plants of this hardwood swamp. If you are in Tampa, don't miss it.

# *Museum of Science and Industry*

**Address:** 4801 East Fowler Avenue, Tampa, FL 33617

**Directions:** From I-75 take exit 54 and continue west on Fowler Avenue (CR 582) for 2.5 miles and follow the signs. The museum will be on your left. From I-275 take exit 34 and go east 3.5 miles on Fowler Avenue.

**Hours:** 9:00 a.m. to 5:00 p.m. Sunday through Thursday; 9:00 a.m. to 7:00 p.m. Friday and Saturday

**Admission fee:** museum only

**Wheelchair access:** yes

**Area:** 1/2 acre

**Phone:** (813) 987-6100

A small butterfly garden and conservatory adjoin the Museum of Science and Industry's futuristic structure. A wide variety of flowering plants that supply nectar to butterflies can be seen here and, of course, many species of native Florida butterflies also make an appearance. Interpretive stations explain the life cycle of butterflies; you will even learn helpful tips on backyard butterfly gardening.

# Sunken Gardens

*This six-acre sinkhole, not far from downtown St. Petersburg, is
the oldest of Florida's botanical gardens and includes thousands of
tropical plants, palms, and orchids.*

**Address:** 1825 4th Street North, St. Petersburg, FL 33704
**Directions:** From I-275 take exit 12 on 22nd Avenue and go east.
Make a right turn onto 4th Street north; the Gardens will be on
your left.
**Hours:** 9:00 a.m. to 5:30 p.m. daily
**Admission fee:** yes
**Wheelchair access:** yes
**Facilities:** gift shop, café
**Area:** 6 acres
**Phone:** (813) 896-3187, (813) 896-3186 for recorded information

Not far from downtown St. Petersburg, a thick wall of tropical vegetation seals off the Sunken Gardens from the
surrounding urban flurry. Upon entering, the visitors find
an entirely different world that lies, at its lowest point, a full fifteen
feet below street level.

When founded in 1903 by George Turner Sr., the Sunken
Gardens were not much more than a sinkhole and a muddy, shallow
lake. Turner used an elaborate drainage system to empty the lake and
the sinkhole of water, revealing a bottom of fertile black marl, a soil
that supports lush plant growth. This six-acre area was first transformed into a small commercial grove of exotic fruit trees. Mr.
Turner's horticultural exploits resulted in the further expansion of the
gardens, which opened in 1935 as a public attraction.

The gardens' winding paths, stream-spanning bridges, quiet
lagoons and cascading waterfalls lend a strong sense of the tropics.
Thousands of tropical plants and trees grow among a canopy of
magnificent **live oaks** (*Quercus virginiana*) and **Australian tree ferns**
(*Cyathea cooperi*). One also encounters wildlife in the walk-through
aviary of exotic birds and in the enclosures alongside the garden
trails. You will see pink flamingos, rainbow-colored macaws, horn-
bills or spoonbills, and alligators.

Several magnificent specimens of **traveller's tree,** rising thirty to forty feet, grow throughout the gardens. The traveller's tree (*Ravenala madagascariensis*), a remarkable relative of the banana family, is widely cultivated throughout the tropics and grown ornamentally in Florida. In its native Madagascar, its wood is used for house construction, its leaves for roofing, the sap yields sugar and its seeds are eaten. Leaves up to ten feet long grow in a flat, fan-shaped cluster on top of the palmlike trunk. It is said that the fan always points in a north-to-south direction like a compass. This is not true, however, and depending on how the tree is planted the leaves may point in any direction. The tree received its common name from its reputation as a source of water for thirsty travelers. A closed cavity at the base of each leaf may hold a quart or more of water; a hole can be drilled in the base of a leaf stalk to obtain the water.

Many tall **royal palms** (*Roystonea regia*), short **bottle palms** (*Hyophorbe lagenicaulis*) and **pony-tail palms** (*Beaucarnea recurvata*) can also be seen here. Another wonder is the hyphenated trunk of **sago palm** (*Cycas circinalis*). **Climbing ferns** (*Stenochloena palustris*), **staghorn ferns** (*Platycerium bifurcatum*) as well as numerous **philo-dendrons, aroids** and **orchids** grow on the ground and also on the trunks or branches of the trees. More than 1,000 orchids grow here, and with 50,000 new flowers planted every year, any season is an enjoyable time to visit.

# Marie Selby Botanical Gardens

*Located on a lovely stretch of Sarasota's waterfront, this eight-acre garden boasts a collection of more than 20,000 different plants and specializes in orchids, bromeliads and aroids. There are twenty distinct garden areas to explore.*

**Address:** 811 South Palm Avenue, Sarasota, FL 34236

**Directions:** From I-75 take exit 39 and go west on Fruitville Road (CR 780) until you reach U.S. 41. Make a left turn on Tamiami Trail (U.S. 41), watch for the Selby Gardens sign, and turn right on South Palm Avenue just after pasing the bayfront marina area.

**Hours:** 10:00 a.m. to 5:00 p.m. daily

**Closed:** Christmas Day

**Admission fee:** yes

**Wheelchair access:** yes

**Facilities:** plant, book and gift shops, snack bar, activities center

**Available:** membership, classes

**Area:** 8 1/2 acres

**Phone:** (941) 366-5730

L ocated on Sarasota's bayfront is the first botanical garden in the world dedicated to the study, research and display of epiphytic plants such as **orchids, bromeliads** and **aroids**. Their mission statement is: "To foster and stimulate understanding and appreciation of tropical plants, with special emphasis on epiphytic plants, through programs of conservation, display, education and research and to provide enjoyment to all who visit the garden."

William and Marie Selby were fascinated by the beauty of
Sarasota and of this part of Florida's Gulf coast. In the early 1920s,
they bought seven acres along Sarasota's bayfront and soon thereafter
built a home among the banyan trees and laurel oaks. This acreage
became the nucleus of the Selby Gardens. In her will, Marie Selby
left the property to the community as a botanical garden "for the
enjoyment of the general public." The Marie Selby Botanical
Gardens were officially opened to the public in 1975 as a not-for-
profit institution.

The Selby Gardens boast a vast living collection of approximately
20,000 plants and 6,000 orchids, displayed in more than 20 distinct
areas. The **Tropical Display House** represents the gardens' prime
display area. Plants are brought here from several research and
growing greenhouses to be exhibited when in peak blooming condition. The temperature, humidity and air movement of this facility
are carefully controlled and continuously adjusted to approximate
conditions in the rain forest. About half of the plants displayed are
epiphytes, with a profusion of thriving **orchids, bromeliads** and
**aroids**.

The **Trellis Walk** just outside the Tropical Display House,
shaded by the **sapodilla tree** (*Manilkara zapota*) and a beautiful
**laurel oak** (*Quercus laurifolia*), contains the more hardy epiphytic
plants. Many **ferns, monsteras** and **calatheas** can be enjoyed in this
area.

A **Banyan Grove** located in the south section of the gardens is
quite impressive. A banyan is a fig tree that develops numerous
aerial roots which grow into the ground from horizontal branches.
These roots eventually grow to become auxiliary trunks that help the
tree to spread outward. In addition to **banyan trees** (*Ficus
benghalensis*), **lofty figs** (*Ficus altissima*) and **Cuban laurels** (*Ficus
retusa*) spread their canopies here. The extensive, above-ground root
system of a **Moreton Bay fig** (*Ficus macrophylla*) is clearly visible.

The **Hibiscus Garden** provides spectacular blossoms to be
enjoyed year-round. A quarter-acre **Cacti and Succulents Garden**
includes species from around the world. The **Bromeliad Display**,
the **Palm Grove and Cycad Collection, Bamboo Pavilion** and
**Tropical Food Garden** also should not be missed.

The Marie Selby Botanical Gardens are not just a showplace for
the thousands of visitors who arrive each year. They have also become

a widely respected center for education and research that includes an Orchid Identification Center and a Bromeliad Identification Center. The Eric Young Micropropagation Center specializes in orchid tissue culture. The Stark Botanical Research Center houses the gardens' research staff and scientific collections.

*Worth Seeing:* The **Museum of Botany and the Arts,** located in the Christy Payne mansion on the grounds of the Selby Gardens, presents a variety of special exhibitions throughout the year.

# Sarasota Jungle Gardens

*Not far from the Sarasota Bayfront, this garden creates a tropical setting with palms, ferns, bromeliads, orchids, and aroids.*

**Address:** 3701 Bayshore Road, Sarasota, FL 34234
**Directions:** Go south on U.S. 41 for 2 miles south of the Sarasota-Bradenton Airport. Make a right turn onto 37th Street and go 2 blocks.
**Hours:** 9:00 a.m. to 5:00 p.m. daily
**Closed:** Christmas Day
**Admission fee:** yes
**Wheelchair access:** yes
**Facilities:** gift shop, café
**Area:** 10 acres
**Phone:** (941) 355-5305

In the 1930s, this ten-acre garden, located close to the Sarasota bayfront, was just a banana grove surrounded by an impenetrable swamp. At that time David B. Lindsey, a local newspaperman, purchased this acreage with the idea of making it into a beautiful botanical garden. In addition to native plants, Lindsey brought tropical plants, flowers and trees from all over the world to create a jungle setting. Lakes, streams and brick paths that twist and turn through the property were added to the design. The Sarasota Jungle Gardens opened as a tourist attraction in 1940.

Jungle trails crossing over small bridges wind past **oaks, palms, pines** and **mahogany trees**. Underneath the canopy thrive **bromeliads, orchids, aroids**, and **ferns**.

The formal gardens are especially beautiful, with lakes surrounded by manicured lawns and palms. Many birds roam through the gardens; some of them are wild and have chosen the gardens as their home, while others, not native to Florida, have been brought here for the enjoyment of visitors. Parrots, flamingos, gallinules, pelicans, seagulls, and peafowl are all an integral part of the gardens.

The visit here is a unique experience, one that will be long remembered.

*Worth Seeing:* **Bird shows** are presented four times daily and
feature cockatoos and macaws, providing entertainment for all ages.
**Reptile shows** are entertaining, as well as educational and even
include a video presentation about the poisonous snakes of Florida.
**The Kiddie Jungle** offers an iguana slide, tiger swings and hounded
tree, and in the **Petting Zoo**, kids of all ages can pet animals or have
their picture taken with a real parrot on their arm.

# Ringling Museums

*The former winter estate of circus tycoon John Ringling features botanical gardens as well as a formal Italian garden.*

**Address:** 5401 Bay Shore Drive, Sarasota, FL 34243
**Directions:** From I-75 take exit 40 and go west on University Parkway for 7 miles. Cross U.S. 41 and follow the short boulevard leading to the museum grounds.
**Hours:** 10:00 a.m. to 5:30 p.m. daily
**Closed:** New Year's Day, Thanksgiving, Christmas Day
**Admission fee:** yes
**Wheelchair access:** partial
**Facilities:** museum shops, café
**Available:** membership
**Area:** 38 acres
**Phone:** (941) 355-5101

Along the shores of Sarasota Bay, just three miles north of downtown Sarasota, the circus owner John Ringling and his wife, Mable, built their winter estate. The opulent thirty-room mansion, **Cá d'Zan** (Venetian dialect for "House of John"), was completed in 1926. The **Art Museum** was completed just south of the house in 1929; its galleries opened to the public in 1930. Upon his death in 1936, Ringling bequeathed the entire estate as well as his art collections to the state of Florida. Soon after the state assumed responsibility for the property in 1946, the **Asolo**, a nineteenth-century Italian theater and a **Circus Museum** were added.

The landscape architecture of the

formal Italian gardens is quite impressive, and the **Sculpture Garden Courtyard** is really memorable. The surrounding botanical gardens contain hundreds of exotic trees, shrubs and flowers, while **palms, banyans** and **bunya bunya** trees are spread throughout the grounds. Lying close to Sarasota Bay are the **Secret Garden** and the **Rose Garden,** with more than 150 hybrids of tea roses. Many statues add beauty and charm to the gardens.

# Sarasota Garden Club

**Address:** 1131 Boulevard of the Arts, Sarasota, FL 34236

**Directions:** From I-75 take exit 39 and go west on Fruitville Road (CR 780) until you reach U.S. 41. Make a right turn and go north on U.S. 41, then turn left on Boulevard of the Arts.

**Hours:** Grounds always open. Inside garden: 9 a.m. to 1 p.m. Monday through Friday

**Closed:** Saturday, Sunday and holidays

**Admission fee:** no

**Wheelchair access:** partial

**Area:** 3 acres

**Phone:** (941) 955-0875

The garden of the Sarasota Garden Club is located not far from the waterfront. Brick pathways will lead you through this mature garden, which was established in 1960. The **Butterfly Garden** offers an array of flowering plants; the **Quiet Garden** invites rest and reflection. The garden features many native and exotic plants, attractive trellises covered by flowering vines and a smaller, fenced-in area with a small pond, waterfall, and water lilies.

# Historic Spanish Point

**Address:** 337 North Tamiami Trail, P.O. Box 846, Osprey, FL
34229
**Directions:** From I-75 take exit 36 (SR 681) to U.S. 41 (Tamiami
Trail) and continue north on U.S. 41 for 5 miles.
**Hours:** 9:00 a.m. to 5:00 p.m. Monday through Saturday; Noon to
5:00 p.m. Sunday
**Closed:** New Year's Day, Easter, Thanksgiving, Christmas Day
**Admission fee:** yes
**Wheelchair access:** partial
**Facilities:** gift shop
**Available:** guided tours
**Area:** 30 acres
**Phone:** (941) 966-5214

Spanish Point was the site of the winter estate of Mrs. Potter
Palmer, a widow of a Chicago tycoon. After acquiring the property in 1910, Mrs. Palmer quickly set to planting, creating
formal lawns and gardens while preserving prehistoric shell middens,
pioneer dwellings, and Indian burial mounds.

Visitors may explore on their own or follow a guided tour
through the formal **Sunken
Garden and Pergola** or
the **Duchene Lawn and
Classic Portal**. A shell
path leads you past the
native vegetation at the
site, which is bordered
by **pine** flatwoods to the
east and **mangroves** to
the west along Little
Sarasota Bay. The
**Cock's Footbridge**
continues on to the **Fern
Walk** or the **Jungle
Walk and Aqueduct**
under a canopy of tall **live oaks, red cedars,** and **mastics.**

# Southwest

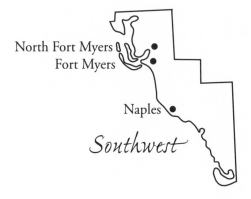

North Fort Myers
Fort Myers

Naples

*Southwest*

# ECHO Gardens

**Address:** 17430 Durrance Road, North Fort Myers, FL 33917

**Directions:** From I-75 take exit 26 and go east for 1 mile on Bayshore Road (CR 78) to Durrance Road, then go north 1/4 mile.

**Hours:** 9:00 a.m. to noon Monday to Saturday

**Closed:** Sundays and holidays

**Admission fee:** donation

**Wheelchair access:** yes

**Available:** free tours Tuesday, Friday, and Saturday at 10:00 a.m.

**Area:** 5 acres

**Phone:** (941) 543-3246

ECHO is an acronym for Educational Concerns for Hunger Organization, a nonprofit Christian organization dedicated to the fight against world hunger. This is accomplished through the dissemination of information and creative ideas, by answering practical farming and gardening questions, and by sending trial packets of seeds of underutilized tropical food plants to 140 countries of the Third World. The organization offers advice on growing traditional food plants in difficult conditions (too dry, too wet or too hilly), and about little-known edible plants.

Just a few minutes from Fort Myers is ECHO's experimental farm and gardens for tropical crops. We were much impressed by their extensive collection of **tropical food plants**, undoubtedly one of the largest in Florida. Visitors may take a free guided tour or wander on their own. Browsing through **Edible Landscape Nursery** will most certainly give you several ideas on how to create an attractive edible landscape in your own backyard. An interesting and thought-provoking garden.

# Edison Winter Home

*The historic winter estate of inventor Thomas Alva Edison includes botanical gardens with more than 1,000 species of plants and a notable collection of palms and cycads.*

**Address:** 2350 McGregor Boulevard, Fort Myers, FL 33901
**Directions:** From I-75 take exit 22 and go west on Colonial Boulevard. After crossing U.S. 41 you reach McGregor Boulevard, where you make a right turn. Continue on McGregor Boulevard until you reach the estate.
**Hours:** 9:00 a.m. to 4:00 p.m. Monday through Saturday; 12:30 p.m. to 4:00 p.m. Sunday
**Closed:** Thanksgiving, Christmas Day
**Admission fee:** yes
**Wheelchair access:** yes
**Facilities:** gift shop, guided tours
**Area:** 14 acres
**Phone:** (941) 334-3614

Thomas Alva Edison's former winter estate spreads over fourteen acres of land on the banks of Caloosahatchee River in the city of Fort Myers. In poor health and invigorated by the Gulf coast's warm climate, Edison soon fell in love with this area. He purchased the land in 1885 and had a home, called Seminole Lodge, and a laboratory constructed the following year. Edison died in 1931; his wife, Mina Edison, deeded the estate to the city of Fort Myers upon her death in 1947.

The talent, vision, and sheer genius of Thomas Edison are well known. His inventions transformed and greatly improved the world we live in and brought him worldwide recognition. There are 1,093 U.S.

patents in his name, and many of these inventions are featured or chronicled in the museum here.

What may not be so commonly known is the fact that Thomas Edison was a master horticulturist and very much interested in botany. The botanical garden he established in Fort Myers contains more than 1,000 varieties of tropical and subtropical plants originating all over the world.

To Edison, who planted much of the collection himself, the garden served many purposes. Of course, he enjoyed the aesthetics of the garden, the beauty of the flowering trees and the taste of many varieties of exotic fruits. But most importantly, the garden provided him with the plant material necessary for some of his experiments. Just consider the following two examples. There are several stands of **giant bamboo** growing wild along the banks of the Caloosahatchee River. After numerous experiments, Edison discovered that carbonized bamboo produced the best electric light filament.

In his search for natural rubber to increase America's rubber supply, Edison experimented with thousands of different plants, finally narrowing his efforts to the common weed called **goldenrod** (*Solidago*). About 125 North American species of goldenrod grow in all sections of the country, most commonly in the Eastern United States. In the wild, this plant is no more than four feet tall, but through cultivation and crossbreeding Edison was able to produce plants more than twelve feet tall and yielding as much as twelve percent rubber. Goldenrod rubber proved to be soft, however, and tires made from it wore out rather quickly. One tire made from goldenrod latex is still on display in the museum more than sixty years later.

One of the many fascinating trees found here is a **banyan tree** (*Ficus benghalensis*). A Florida champion tree since 1980, this specimen has a circumference of more than 400 feet. It was brought from India and given to Thomas Edison by Harvey Firestone in 1925, at which time the tree was only four feet tall and two inches in diameter.

The collection of **palms** and **cycads** is also certainly worth exploring.

*Worth Seeing:*

**Museum**. Countless displays of memorabilia related to the life of Thomas Alva Edison.

**Chemical Laboratory**. Here Edison worked on his research of goldenrod as a source of natural rubber. The laboratory remains in the same condition he left it.

**Seminole Lodge**. Edison's Victorian home is furnished with early American furniture. The original carbon-filament light bulbs made by Edison are still in use.

**The Mangoes**. Next door to the Seminole Lodge is the meticulously restored winter home of Henry Ford, a good friend of Edison's.

# Fragrance Garden

**Address:** 7330 Gladiolus Drive, Fort Myers, FL 33908
**Directions:** From I-75 take exit 21 and go west on Daniels Parkway.
Turn south on Six Mile Cypress Parkway (CR 808) and continue
past U.S. 41. Lakes Park will be on your right.
**Hours:** 8:00 a.m. to 6:00 p.m. daily
**Admission fee:** no
**Wheelchair access:** yes
**Area:** 2 acres
**Phone:** (941) 432-2004

This garden, located within Lee County Lakes Park, is a pleasant surprise. It is a true "touch and smell" garden with a multitude of native and exotic fragrant plants. Watch butterflies sample the nectar of flowering plants in the **Butterfly Garden**. Touch and smell the herbs in the elevated herb planters stretching from the entrance chickee all the way to the sundial. Trees and shrubs line the **Memory Lane**. The 170-foot **Vine Arbor** is covered with flowering and fruiting vines. The **Tropical Fruit and Spice Walk** features exotic fruit trees. The **Cactus and Succulents Garden** with its array of arid desert plants is quite pleasing; a gazebo in the center invites you to sit down and admire it all.

# Caribbean Gardens

**Address:** 1590 Goodlette-Frank Road, Naples, FL 34102

Directions: From I-75 take exit 16 and go west on Pine Ridge Road (CR 896) for 2.5 miles. Make a left turn on Goodlette Road (CR 851) and go 3 miles. The gardens will be on your left.

**Hours:** 9:30 a.m. to 5:30 p.m. daily

**Closed:** Easter, Thanksgiving, Christmas Day

**Admission fee:** yes

**Wheelchair access:** yes

**Facilities:** gift shop, Bamboo Café.

**Available:** boat tour

**Area:** 52 acres

**Phone:** (941) 262-5409

Dr. Henry Nehrling founded the Caribbean Gardens in Naples in 1919. The gardens were his dream tropical garden where rare plants from all over the world could grow. By constantly enlarging his already impressive collection with additional specimens, Nehrling eventually brought the total to more than 3,000 species. But after his death in 1929, his gardens grew wild and untended for the next two decades.

Julius Fleischmann, who discovered the neglected gardens in the early 1950s, was able to visualize their full potential. After acquiring the property, he restored the site by planting new species and building new trails and lakes. Caribbean Gardens first opened to the public in 1954 and quickly became immensely popular with visitors. After Fleischmann's death, world traveler and expedition leader Colonel Lawrence "Jungle Larry" Tetzlaff and his wife Nancy "Safari Jane" Tetzlaff relocated their collection of rare and endangered animals to the gardens, thus creating a true botanical and zoological garden. The gardens are constantly expanding their exhibits and educational programs and present a unique opportunity to see rare and endangered animals in a tropical setting.

*Worth Seeing:* The guided **Primate Expedition Cruise** will take you on a boat tour of Lake Victoria observing apes, lemurs and monkeys in their island habitats.

# Southeast

Southeast

West Palm Beach

Palm Beach

Coconut
Creek

Delray Beach

Davie

Fort Lauderdale
North Miami Beach

Miami
Coral Gables
Coconut Grove
Homestead

# Mounts Botanical Garden

*A 14-acre botanical garden, the largest in Palm Beach County, displays more than 2,000 plants.*

**Address:** 531 North Military Trail, West Palm Beach, FL 33415
**Directions:** From I-95 take the exit at Southern Boulevard and go west to Military Trail. There make a right turn (north). The entrance to the Garden is on your left behind the Agricultural Building.
**Hours:** 8:30 a.m. to 4:30 p.m. Monday to Saturday; 1:00 p.m. to 5:00 p.m. Sunday; 1:00 p.m. to 5:00 p.m. legal holidays
**Closed:** New Year's Day, Thanksgiving, Christmas Day
**Admission fee:** donation
**Wheelchair access:** yes
**Facilities:** garden shop
**Available:** membership, lectures, classes. Guided tours 11:00 a.m. Saturday, 2:30 p.m. Sunday
**Area:** 14 acres
**Phone:** (561) 233-1749

The Mounts Botanical Garden located in West Palm Beach is Palm Beach County's oldest and largest botanical garden. The garden was started under a program of the Palm Beach County Cooperative Extension Service to help the public understand the intricacies of South Florida gardening and to enhance plant appreciation in general. In 1954 Marvin "Red" Mounts, then the County Agricultural Extension agent, started the program by planting tropical trees in the acreage adjacent to the Extension office. His efforts were supported by various government and educational entities, garden clubs, plant societies, and dedicated individuals. At the present time there are more than 2,000 different plants thriving in the garden.

In the **Shade and Flowering Tree Area** a beautiful specimen of **royal poinciana** (*Delonix regia*) can be found. A Madagascar native, the royal poinciana is certainly one of the most beautiful and flamboyant tropical trees. When blossoming in May or June, the tree is covered with flowers, each with one striped petal, in varying tones of red and orange. This display of color may last up to four months. The poinciana prefers full sun for best flowering and thrives in areas with wet and dry seasons.

You can also see **eucalyptus** in this section. There are over 500 species of eucalyptus, which is native to Australia. The eucalyptus grows up to 300 feet high, making it one of the tallest trees in Australia and in the world. Young eucalyptus trees have foliage that is different in shape, size, color, and arrangement from that of a mature tree. It is therefore very difficult, if not impossible, to identify a young eucalyptus tree. The trees constantly shed strips of bark; the bark peels as the tree matures. **Rainbow bark eucalyptus** (*Eucalyptus deglupta*) is a very tall tree with fascinating peeling bark of many colors. **Lemon eucalyptus** (*Eucalyptus citriododra*), another tall tree, has lemon-scented leaves. The wood of some eucalyptus trees also has a pleasant fragrance. Eucalyptus oil is made out of the leaves, roots and bark and has germicidal properties.

The Mounts Garden also includes a **Palm Collection; Citrus, Banana, and Tropical Fruit Collections; Native and Poisonous Plant Collections;** a **Rain Forest Exhibit; Begonia and Rose Collections;** a **Hibiscus Collection;** a **Bougainvillea Arbor; Aquatic Plantings;** and even an aromatic **Herb Garden.**

# Ann Norton Sculpture Gardens

**Address:** 253 Barcelona Road, West Palm Beach, FL 33401

**Directions:** From I-95 take exit 52 and go east on Okeechobee
Boulevard to South Flagler Drive. Make a right turn on Flagler
Drive and go south 1/2 mile to Barcelona Road.

**Hours:** October 1 to May 15: 10:00 a.m. to 4:00 p.m.

**Closed:** Sunday and Monday

**Admission fee:** yes

**Wheelchair access:** partial

**Area:** 1.7 acres

**Phone:** (561) 832-5328

On the Intracoastal Waterway, near downtown West Palm Beach, are the former residence and gardens of the prominent sculptor Ann Weaver Norton. Several smaller connecting gardens provide the perfect surroundings or backdrop for the artist's original sculptures, more than 100 of which are displayed in the gardens and house. We found the impressive **palm** collection an unexpected surprise. Large **live oaks** provide shade for **orchids**, **bromeliads**, **ferns**, and **aroids**. The house is listed in the National Register of Historic Places.

# Norton Museum of Art

**Address:** 1451 South Olive Avenue, West Palm Beach, FL 33401

**Directions:** From I-95 take exit 52 and go east on Okeechobee Boulevard to South Olive Avenue.

**Hours:** 10:00 a.m. to 5:00 p.m. Monday to Saturday; 1:00 p.m. to 5:00 p.m. Sunday

**Closed:** major holidays

**Admission fee:** yes

**Wheelchair access:** yes

**Area:** 1 1/2 acres

**Phone:** (561) 832-5196

When in the Palm Beach area, the Norton Museum of Art is a must. The art exhibits here will astound you. When you need a place to relax, there is a central sculpture garden as well as two additional small gardens on the east and west sections of the museum grounds. You will enjoy the **palms** and **heather**.

# Society of the Four Arts Botanical and Sculpture Gardens

*Several small and intimate gardens in the Four Arts Plaza offer palms, exotic tropical trees, flowering vines, orchids, and bromeliads.*

**Address:** 2 Four Arts Plaza, Palm Beach, FL 33480

**Directions:** From I-95 or from the Florida Turnpike take the Okeechobee Boulevard exit and go east all the way over the Royal Palm Bridge. Take a left turn past the bridge on Lake Drive.

**Hours:** November 1 to April 30: 10:00 a.m. to 5:00 p.m. Monday through Friday; 9:00 a.m. to 1:00 p.m. Saturday. May 1 to October 31: 10:00 a.m. to 5:00 p.m. Monday through Friday

**Closed:** Sundays and major holidays

**Admission fee:** no

**Wheelchair access:** yes

**Area:** 3 acres

**Phone:** (561) 655-2766

L ocated directly in the city of Palm Beach are the intimate yet beautiful Botanical Gardens of the Society of the Four Arts. The Society of the Four Arts is a nonprofit organization which was incorporated in 1936 to promote the appreciation of art, music, drama and literature. The gardens are adjacent to the Four Arts Library and Sculpture Garden at the Four Arts Plaza and are maintained by The Garden Club of Palm Beach. They originated with seven small demonstration gardens that were planted here in 1938. These gardens were originally intended to assist new home owners in selecting plants and landscaping materials suitable for the south Florida climate.

The entrance to the gardens is either from the west, through the main gate from the Four Arts Plaza, or from the east, from the **Sculpture Garden**. Either way, you will be facing the **Boxwood Garden** upon entering. North of the Boxwood Garden is a patio area with large **fishtail palms** (*Caryota mitis*) growing at the corners of the library building. A beautiful **bleeding heart vine** (*Clerodendrum*

*thomsoniae*) with its delicate
white and red blossoms thrives
on a sun-exposed wall. The
adjacent **Rose Garden** contains
several varieties of roses that add
color and beauty to the garden
year-round. The **Herb Garden**
under the **strawberry guava
tree** (*Psidium littorale*) is
replanted each spring and fall.

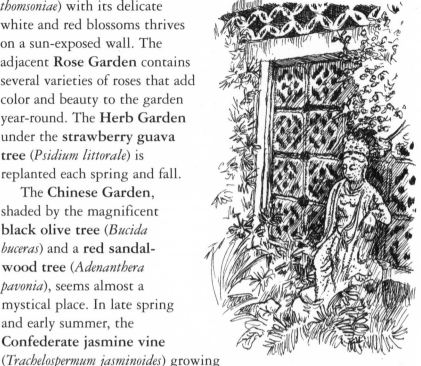

The **Chinese Garden**,
shaded by the magnificent
**black olive tree** (*Bucida
buceras*) and a **red sandal-
wood tree** (*Adenanthera
pavonia*), seems almost a
mystical place. In late spring
and early summer, the
**Confederate jasmine vine**
(*Trachelospermum jasminoides*) growing
over the south wall displays brilliant, delightfully fragrant white
flowers. A plaque on one of the side walls of the garden describes the
Chinese concept of a garden: "To the Chinese the making of a garden
is the effort of the individual to attain unity with the universe. In its
inception the garden was a retreat. In China it was essentially an aid
to contemplation. Exalted by beauty, lulled by its harmony, the
Chinese were able to comprehend truths beyond ordinary perception.
A quiet space in which one found relief from tension. In the design
for contentment which is the basis of Chinese philosophy, every individual possesses that which in his own mind is a garden. The
Chinese feel that unless a man has a garden, he scarcely grasps the
reason for existence."

In the **Moonlight Garden** one can admire **giant crinum lilies**
(*Crinum jagus 'Giganteum'*) and **ginger lilies** (*Alpinia zerumbet*) against
the background of **areca palms** (*Dypsis lutescens*) and **emerald ferns**
(*Asparagus densiflorus*). Traditionally, plants with white blossoms were
selected for moon gardens because they can perfectly reflect the
moonlight. Many of these flowering plants are also heavily fragrant,
further adding to the experience.

Cummer Museum of Art and Gardens
Jacksonville

Maclay State Gardens
Tallahassee

Venetian Pool, Coral Gables

Maitland Art Center, Maitland

Tropical water lilies; Fairchild Tropical Garden
Miami

Fountain garden; Vizcaya Museum and Gardens, Miami

Ormond Memorial Art Museum and Gardens, Ormond Beach

Above:
Boxwood garden;
Society of the
Four Arts
Botanical and
Sculpture Garden,
Palm Beach

Right:
Reflection pool;
Bok Tower
Gardens,
Lake Wales

Marie Selby Botanical Gardens
Sarasota

Palms in the lowlands; Fairchild Tropical Garden
Miami

Ringling Museums
Sarasota

Cypress Gardens, Winter Haven

Washington Oaks State Gardens, Palm Coast

Morikami Museum and Japanese Gardens, Delray Beach

Audubon House and Tropical Gardens, Key West

Oldest House
St. Augustine

Chinese garden; Society of the Four Arts Botanical and Sculpture Garden
Palm Beach

The Ancient Spanish Monastery of St. Bernard de Clairvaux
North Miami Beach

Historic Spanish Point, Osprey

The south section of the gardens encompasses the **Palm Garden, Fountain Garden, Madonna Garden, Tropical Garden, Spanish Patio Garden, Jungle Garden** and **Rock Garden**. A multitude of **palms**, exotic tropical trees, **ferns, aroids,** and **bromeliads** can be enjoyed throughout the gardens; stone patios, walkways, and pathways accentuate the tranquil setting.

# Pan's Garden

**Address:** 386 Hibiscus Avenue, Palm Beach, FL 33480
**Directions:** From I-95 take exit 52 and go east on Okeechobee
   Boulevard. Three blocks after the bridge turn right (south) on
   Hibiscus Avenue.
**Hours:** 9:00 a.m. to 5:00 p.m. daily
**Closed:** holidays
**Admission fee:** no
**Wheelchair access:** yes
**Facilities:** none
**Area:** 1/2 acre
**Phone:** (561) 832-0731

This small but beautiful garden opened in Palm Beach in 1994. Named after Pan, the Greek god of fields and flocks, it is planted entirely with plants indigenous to the Palm Beach area. Everything seems carefully balanced between upland and wetland areas. It is a young garden, but it is easy to visualize its beauty when the oaks and cypress will really spread their canopies. A Mediterranean-style pavilion and a pergola add further dimension to the landscape. With each passing year this garden will get even better.

# Cluett Memorial Gardens

**Address:** 141 S. Country Road, Palm Beach, FL 33480
**Directions:** From I-95 take exit 52 and go east on Okeechobee
   Boulevard, across the bridge to Royal Palm Way to Country
   Road. Go north for about 1/4 mile.
**Hours:** 8:00 a.m. to 5:00 p.m. daily.
**Admission fee:** no
**Wheelchair access:** yes
**Area:** 1 acre
**Phone:** (561) 655-4554

These formal gardens on the grounds of Bethesda-by-the-Sea Church offer beautiful flowering trees, reflecting pools. A very quiet and peaceful place.

# Morikami Museum and Japanese Gardens

*Acres of tranquil pine forests, lakes, nature trails, Japanese gardens, and a rare bonsai collection.*

**Address:** 4000 Morikami Road, Delray Beach, FL 33446

**Directions:** From the Florida Turnpike take exit 81 and go east on Atlantic Avenue (Rt. 806). Make a right turn (south) on Jog Road and continue until making a right turn on Morikami Road. From I-95 take Linton Boulevard, make a left turn (south) on Jog Road, then make a right turn on Morikami Road.

**Hours:** Museum: 10:00 a.m. to 5:00 p.m. daily. Morikami Park is open seven days a week, including holidays, from sunrise to sunset, with free admission.

**Closed:** Museum: Mondays, New Year's Day, Easter, Fourth of July, Thanksgiving, Christmas Day

**Admission fee:** yes

**Wheelchair access:** yes

**Facilities:** museum store, library, café, snack bar, tea house

**Available:** membership, classes, lectures

**Area:** 200 acres

**Phone:** (561) 495-0233

Secluded in a quiet area of Palm Beach County are 200 acres of peaceful serenity called the Morikami Museum and Japanese Gardens.

At the beginning of this century, a small group of pioneering Japanese farmers settled in this area. With the assistance of Henry Flagler's Land Company, they started an agricultural community, calling it the Yamato Colony after a word for ancient Japan. Growing primarily pineapples, the settlers endured crop failures, hurricanes, heat and everything else nature could dish out for twenty years. Finally, the harsh life took its toll. One by one, they gave up and left for more hospitable regions of this country, or they returned home to Japan.

One colonist remained, never giving up, continuing to work his

pineapple fields. This was George Sukeji
Morikami, who eventually pros-
pered and amassed several
hundred acres of land. In 1974,
two years before his death,
George Morikami donated 200
acres of his land to Palm Beach
County. He wished for a park,
gardens, and a museum to
be developed on this land to
enhance understanding
between the Japanese and
American people. His wish
became reality in 1977 when
the Morikami Park, Museum
and Gardens opened to the
public.

**Yamato-kan**, the original museum building, is situated on the
island in the Morikami Pond. This structure, fashioned after a
Japanese home, is centered around an open courtyard garden and
features as a permanent exhibit a turn-of-the-century farming
community. A major new building, opened in 1993, houses additional exhibit galleries, a library, and classrooms.

The **Japanese Garden** surrounding the Yamato-kan on the island
is easily accessible by a wooden footbridge. The garden's combination
of plants, rocks, and water is quite pleasing, and the **Pebble-garden
Courtyard** inside of the Yamato-kan is intriguing.

The rare **Bonsai Collection** features Florida native trees in minia-
ture. A waterfall cascades into a lake that holds colorful **pond lilies**
as well as ornamental Japanese carp or Koi.

The gardens are linked by a one-mile nature trail that meanders
through the stands of **pine, bamboo** and **cypress**. The pleasing
fragrance of pines coupled with the feeling of peacefulness make this
walk especially enjoyable.

*Worth Seeing:* The **Morikami Museum**, a new 32,000-sq.-foot
facility which includes exhibition galleries, theater, library,
Infotronic Gallery and classrooms.

# Butterfly World

*The largest and most complete butterfly facility in the world also features beautiful botanical gardens with one of the largest collections of passion vines.*

**Address:** 3600 West Sample Road, Coconut Creek, FL 33073
**Directions:** From I-95 go west on Sample Road for about 4 miles. From the Florida Turnpike go about 1/2 mile west on Sample Road.
**Hours:** 9:00 a.m. to 5:00 p.m. Monday to Saturday, 1:00 p.m. to 5:00 p.m. Sunday
**Closed:** Thanksgiving, Christmas Day
**Admission fee:** yes
**Wheelchair access:** yes
**Facilities:** gift shop, plant shop, café
**Area:** 3 acres
**Phone:** (954) 977-4400 and (954) 977-4434

For lovers of flowers and/or butterflies, Butterfly World is a treat. Not only can one enjoy in amazement thousands upon thousands of butterflies, but the grounds of Butterfly World contain some of the most beautiful flowering gardens found in Florida.

Butterfly World opened its doors in 1988 as the first center for butterflies in the United States. At the time of this writing, it remains the largest and most complete facility in the world dedicated to the preservation of butterflies and their habitats.

The plants grown and displayed here serve a dual purpose: they must be beautiful as well as functional. They are here to please the eyes and to provide everything needed for the life cycle of the butterfly. In order to understand the subtle intricacies of a butterfly's life cycle, consider the following facts:

Adult butterflies need nectar from flowering plants as a food
source.

Different species of butterflies prefer different species of flowers.

Most nectar plants have large and brightly colored flowers; certain
butterflies prefer a particular color of blossoms. This favorite
color can change with the species and the age of the butterfly.

The plant food sources for caterpillars are quite varied but not
necessarily the same as those used by adult butterflies as a
source of nectar.

Most species of butterflies will lay eggs only on one species of
plant. Once the eggs hatch, the larvae begin to feed on the
host plant.

Can you see what it takes to create a butterfly habitat? Thousands
of specialized plants must be grown, so that their leaves can serve as
food for the caterpillars and their blossoms can provide the nectar for
adult butterflies.

The various displays and sections of Butterfly World will challenge
your imagination. The **Tropical Rain Forest** exhibit is a dreamlike
walk among lush tropical vegetation: **bromeliads, orchids, ferns**
and **aroids,** with butterflies feeding on the blossoms or just landing
on your head or shoulder for a few seconds.

Outside of the screened **Aviary Gardens**, native butterflies fly
and feed everywhere. In the **Secret Garden** a mazelike structure of
trellises covered by a profusion of flowering vines can be admired.
One of the world's largest collections of flowering **passion vines** is
here (*Passiflora coccinea*, *Passiflora incense,* and *Passiflora maliformis,* just
to mention a few), as well as large collections of *Thumbergias*,
*Cassias,* and *Stachytarphetas.*

The collection of **Aristolochias,** or "Dutchman's Pipe Vines," is
quite extensive. These generally poisonous vines are used by many
butterflies as hosts for their caterpillars. Their flowers manifest some
of the most unusual shapes in the plant world. Some look like pipes,
some like birds. Others resemble pouches hanging from the plant.
*Aristolochia grandiflora*, *Aristolochia ringens* (also called **pelican
flower**), *Aristolochia trifecta*, *Aristolochia gilbertii,* and *Aristolochia
maxima* can be viewed here.

The **English Rose Garden** showcases about twenty varieties of
roses of various colors and fragrances. A beautiful collection of **water
lilies** is scattered all over the lake.

# Bonnet House

**Address:** 900 North Birch Road, Fort Lauderdale, FL 33304

**Directions:** From I-95 take exit 30 and go east on Sunrise Boulevard for 4 miles. After the second bridge, make a right turn on Birch Road.

**Hours:** 10:00 a.m. to 2:00 p.m. Wednesday to Friday; noon to 2:00 p.m. Saturday and Sunday

**Closed:** Monday, Tuesday, and holidays

**Admission fee:** yes

**Wheelchair access:** yes

**Facilities:** gift shop

**Available:** membership

**Area:** 35 acres

**Phone:** (954) 563-5393

Situated on the Fort Lauderdale waterfront, Bonnet House was the winter residence of artists Frederic and Evelyn Bartlett. The plantation-style house was completed in 1921. Pleased with the tropical vegetation that surrounded him and that provided his greatest inspiration, Bartlett added many new plantings to provide additional color and fragrance to the landscape. Filled with art and personal mementos, the house blends art, architecture, and history. Evelyn Bartlett donated the property to the Florida Trust for Historic Preservation in 1983.

Not much has changed on the Bonnet House property since the 1920s, allowing visitors to see and experience a long-lost south Florida lifestyle. Lush tropical vegetation flourishes in a natural setting. There is a **Desert Garden** and a **Citrus Grove,** palm-lined ponds, and a **Ficus Tunnel.** The **Island Theater** is surrounded by a coconut palm–lined moat stocked with Koi. A pavilion overlooks the **Lily Pond,** and on the south end of the estate a fountain marks the end of the tree-lined **Allee.** The **Orchid House** displays a very respectable orchid collection with more than 1,500 plants. The **Nature Trail** will lead you through several native plant communities. Listed in the National Register of Historic Places.

# Flamingo Gardens

*These botanical gardens have outstanding displays of tropical and subtropical plants, the largest collection of Champion trees in the state of Florida, and excellent heliconia and ginger collections.*

**Address:** 3750 Flamingo Road, Davie/Fort Lauderdale, FL 33330

**Directions:** From I-95 in Fort Lauderdale take exit 26 AB to I-595 and go west. After almost 8 miles turn on Flamingo Road and after going south about 3 miles you will see the gardens on your left.

**Hours:** 9:30 a.m. to 5:30 p.m. daily

**Closed:** Thanksgiving, Christmas Day and Mondays from June 1 to September 30

**Admission fee:** yes

**Wheelchair access:** yes

**Facilities:** garden and gift shops, grill, Fresh Fruit Patio

**Area:** 60 acres total; gardens, 12 acres.

**Phone:** (954) 473-2955

L ocated in Broward County just southwest of Fort Lauderdale, the Flamingo Gardens provide a calm, quiet respite in rapidly developing south Florida.

The present Flamingo Gardens are situated on the site of the old Flamingo Groves, citrus groves incorporated by Floyd L. Wray in 1926. Although citrus was Wray's main interest and fascination, in 1932 he established his arboretum: a twelve-acre botanical garden devoted to rare subtropical and tropical trees and shrubs. Soon thereafter Flamingo Groves was selected by the Department of Agriculture Plant Introduction Board as a site for the study of tropical trees.

flamingo

After Floyd L. Wray's death his wife, Jane, created the Floyd L. Wray Memorial Foundation, which became the driving force behind the development of a botanical garden. Membership in the gardens was opened to the public in 1985. Today, the foundation still owns and operates Flamingo Gardens.

How better to summarize what Flamingo Gardens is all about than to quote their own statement of purpose: "It is the intent of Flamingo Gardens to depict and maintain for posterity the natural and cultural heritage of South Florida and the Everglades by preserving and displaying in a living museum an outstanding collection of tropical and subtropical plants and birds native to the area, presented in naturalistic habitats, as well as the cultural artifacts of early South Florida settlers and native peoples. These exhibits are maintained and presented in order to encourage environmental awareness in visiting tourists, area residents and school children; to increase knowledge and interest in the agricultural and horticultural history of our region; to provide a repository for endangered plant and bird species and a living library of specific taxa available for research and education; and to breed and release into the wild native South Florida birds. It is the further intent to inspire an appreciation for the beauty and diversity of tropical and subtropical plants from around the world that can be grown in our area, and to guide the public in environmentally responsible and aesthetic horticultural practices. Finally, we wish to provide a calm oasis of natural beauty within the increasingly urban South Florida community."

### Main Sections of the Gardens

The **Arboretum** proudly displays many Champion trees, meaning the largest known trees of their kind in Florida. A Champion is determined by calculating its height, spread and girth; it is verified by the State of Florida Division of Forestry. A tree will remain a Champion tree until a larger specimen is found. The largest collection of Champion trees in Florida, numbering twenty-two, can be found right here in Flamingo Gardens, with two of the trees being the largest of their kind in the continental United States. Here are just four of them:

- The **cluster fig** (*Ficus racemosa*), a 108-foot giant measuring 45 feet in circumference, and the **dynamite** or **sandbox tree** (*Hura crepitans*) are the largest of their kind in the continental United States.
- The **Panama candle tree** (*Parmentiera cereifera*), native to

Central America, is named for the elongated, dangling yellow fruit resembling yellow candles. The candles are preceded by clusters of white, bell-shaped flowers growing directly out of the trunk and branches.

- The **yellow poinciana** (*Peltophorum pterocarpum*), a native of Sri Lanka and Northern Australia, stands more than seventy-five feet tall. This stately, rapidly growing, very ornamental tree is a close relative of the royal poinciana. Small, yellow flowers usually cover the entire canopy; the most intense colors are present from May to September.

Beneath the shady canopy of the giant trees are the **heliconia** and **ginger** collections as well as the **Bromeliad Garden**. The gardens also serve as an official repository for the collection of heliconias for the International Heliconia Society.

One can enjoy the **Flowering Tree Walk, Rare Fruit Collection, Banana Plantation,** and **Rainforest Area.** The **Hibiscus** and **Iris Gardens** as well as the **Xeriscape,** and **Butterfly** and **Hummingbird Gardens,** are worth an exploration. Many varieties of orchids are displayed in the **Tropical Plant House.**

Don't forget to visit the **Native Hammock,** the **Wetlands,** and **Citrus Groves.** The gardens' tram will take you on a narrated tour right into the heart of the citrus groves and the hammocks.

*Worth Seeing:*

The **Historic Wray Home,** on Pine Island Ridge, sits under 200-year-old live oaks. The House was restored to its original 1930s state.

The **Everglades Museum** features prehistoric Indian and Seminole artifacts.

The **"Free Flight Aviary"** is home to more than ninety species of native South Florida birds. It provides needed care for injured and sick birds, with the main goal being their return to the wild. Different plant communities are included in the aviary: coastal prairie, sawgrass prairie, cypress forest, subtropical hardwood hammock and mangrove swamp. The aviary is the breeding center for the endangered wood stork and roseate spoonbill; the largest U.S. captive collection of wading birds is here as well.

The **Bird of Prey Center**, one of the newer additions, opened in 1990 and is home to birds that were either handraised or injured and would be unable to survive in the wild if released.

The **Flamingo Pond** includes three species of flamingo: Caribbean, Lesser African and Greater African.

The **Everglades Wildlife Sanctuary** with alligators and otters.

The artificial 1.6-acre **Wetlands** attracting herons, ibis, wood storks, and ospreys.

# Ancient Spanish Monastery of St. Bernard de Clairvaux ✤

**Address:** 16711 W. Dixie Highway, North Miami Beach, FL 33160
**Directions:** From I-95 take exit 19 and go east 3 miles on Miami
  Gardens Drive, then make a right turn on West Dixie Highway.
**Hours:** 10:00 a.m. to 4:00 p.m. Monday through Saturday; Noon to
  4:00 p.m. Sunday
**Admission fee:** yes
**Wheelchair access:** yes
**Area:** 6 acres
**Phone:** (305) 945-1461

A great deal of history goes with the Monastery of St. Bernard de Clairvaux. Originally built in Sacramenia, a province of Segovia, Spain, in the 1130s, it was occupied by Cistercian monks for almost 700 years. During the social upheavals of that period, the cloisters and monastery were seized, sold, and converted into a granary and stables in the 1830s. Purchased by William Randolph Hearst in 1925, the buildings were dismantled stone by stone, packed in 11,000 wooden crates cushioned with hay, and properly labeled for identification, and then shipped to the United States. Unfortunately, at just about the same time an epidemic of hoof-and-mouth disease was spreading in Segovia province. The U.S. Department of Agriculture ordered the entire shipment quarantined. All of the crates were opened; the hay, a possible carrier of the disease, was burned. But the workers did not properly replace the

stones in their appropriate crates.

Hearst's financial problems forced him to sell most of his collection, and the stones were stored in a Brooklyn warehouse for twenty-six years. In 1952, the stones were purchased by a pair of businessmen for use as a tourist attraction in Florida. It took almost two years and $1.5 million to put this mislabeled puzzle back together. When the monastery was finally reassembled, a large number of stones still could not be matched. Some were used in the construction of the present Church's Parish Hall, and others remain stored on the back of the property. The monastery was eventually acquired by the Episcopal Church.

The formal gardens with their clipped hedges and brick walkways are quite pleasing. Under the canopy of large **live oaks** a multitude of **palms, philodendrons, orchids,** and **bromeliads** thrive. Before the monastery was reassembled, the site was a nursery, and nearly 1,000 plants and trees still remain from that era. Listed in the National Register of Historic Places.

# Vizcaya Museum and Gardens

*A spectacular formal garden surrounds Vizcaya, the winter retreat of industrialist James Deering. In addition to the main garden, there are several smaller gardens to see.*

**Address:** 3251 South Miami Avenue, Miami, FL 33129
**Directions:** Take I-95 south to exit 1 and follow signs to Vizcaya, or take U.S. 1 to SW 17th Avenue, go east and follow the signs to Vizcaya.
**Hours:** 9:30 a.m. to 5:00 p.m. daily
**Closed:** Christmas Day
**Admission fee:** yes
**Wheelchair access:** first floor only, most of the gardens
**Facilities:** gift shop, café
**Available:** guided tours, group tours by appointment
**Area:** 30 acres
**Phone:** (305) 250-9133

Overlooking Biscayne Bay, Vizcaya provides a unique glimpse of a lifestyle that is no more. The house was built in the years 1914 to 1916 as a winter retreat for the industrialist James Deering of International Harvester, who named the estate after a Basque word meaning "elevated place."

Three different architects created Vizcaya in the style of Italian Renaissance villas. F. Burrall Hoffman designed the buildings, Diego Suarez designed the gardens and Paul Chalfin was the project's general artistic supervisor. The villa itself has thirty-four rooms, all arranged around a central courtyard and furnished with an exquisite collection of sixteenth- through nineteenth-century European art and furnishing.

When Vizcaya's gardens were completed in 1921, the entire estate comprised 180 acres, including a small, imitation northern Italian farm village.

James Deering's death in 1925 and a devastating hurricane in 1926 were severe blows to Vizcaya. Its future was uncertain until 1952, when Dade County acquired the property. After extensive renovations the villa and about thirty remaining acres were opened

to the public as a museum.
Today Vizcaya is a
National Historic
Landmark.
The formal gardens
adjoining the
south side of
the villa
combine
sixteenth-
century Italian
Renaissance and
seventeenth-
century French

Baroque, classical European styles adapted to the subtropical climate.
Diego Suarez conceived the gardens as a spacious outdoor room,
backed by forests and divided into smaller gardens by vegetation and
architectural features, including fountains, reflecting pools, cascades,
trimmed hedges, decorative urns, balustrades and sculpture.

The **Main Garden,** with its semicircular pools, central island and
statue-lined walks, stretches from the villa to the Mount and Casino
at the south end of the property. Smaller gardens include the
**Fountain Garden** to the east of the Mount, the **Maze Garden,**
lined by hedges of **orange jasmine** (*Murraya paniculata*), the
**Theater Garden** and the **Secret Garden.** The **Gimbel Garden** for
the blind contains plants selected for their texture or aroma.

The **Hammock Trail** meanders through the native, coastal hardwood hammock and affords a view of what south Florida looked like
before development and "progress" wiped out much of it.

# Fairchild Tropical Garden

*The Fairchild Tropical Garden is one of the world's preeminent
botanical gardens, with eighty-three acres of palms, cycads, flowering trees, bamboos, flowering vines, bromeliads, ferns, and
orchids. The collection of some 800 species of palms is generally
recognized as the most important documented palm collection in
the world.*

**Address:** 10901 Old Cutler Road, Miami, FL 33156
**Directions:** From U.S. 1 go east on Kendall Dr. (88th St.) to Old
    Cutler Rd. and continue south to the garden. Or take LeJeune
    Ave. (42nd Ave.) south to Old Cutler Road and continue south to
    the garden.
**Hours:** 9:30 a.m. to 4:30 p.m. daily
**Closed:** Christmas Day
**Admission fee:** yes
**Wheelchair access:** yes
**Facilities:** garden shop, café, snack bar
**Available:** membership, tram tours, guided walking tours, classes,
    lectures, workshops
**Area:** 83 acres
**Phone:** (305) 667-1651

Located just a few miles from downtown Miami, the Fairchild
Tropical Garden spreads over eighty-three acres and includes
the largest collection of **palms, cycads, tropical,** and
**subtropical plants** in the continental United States.

In the 1930s, Colonel Robert H. Montgomery, an avid amateur
plant collector, envisioned a tropical garden in southern Florida, the
only region in the continental United States where tropical and subtropical plants can grow throughout the year. Since his own palm
and cycad collection had already generated much interest, he
believed a tropical garden would appeal to and be supported by the
public.

Colonel Montgomery was encouraged by, among others, his close
friend Dr. David Fairchild, for whom the garden was later named.
One of the most noted and respected American plant explorers of his

time, Dr. Fairchild enjoyed worldwide recognition as a botanist. He created and headed the U.S. Department of Agriculture "Seed and Plant Introduction Section" and introduced more than 2,000 varieties of plants, fruit, trees, grains and vegetables into this country.

The renowned Harvard-educated landscape architect William Lyman Phillips was retained to create the garden's design. At the time he was superintendent of the Civilian Conservation Corps in southern Florida, which later did much of the original excavation and construction.

The layout of the garden is based on ecological communities (where plants share the same habitat) and on taxonomic plots, which include plant species belonging to the same families. The wide open spaces, lakes and plant groupings provided diverse scenery within a classic architectural design.

After several years of planning and work, Colonel Montgomery realized his dream when Fairchild Tropical Garden opened in 1938. Since that time, the garden has displayed tropical and subtropical plants and has promoted botanical research and conservation to educate scientists and the public.

### A Tour of the Garden

Pathways wind through the garden's eighty-three acres, but many visitors choose to start their exploration by taking a guided tram tour. The trained guides combine botanical and historical information in the two-mile tour. Visitors may also leave the beaten path and explore at their own pace to smell the flowers, touch the leaves and bark of unusual trees, or just admire the surrounding beauty.

The Fairchild Tropical Garden is home to the largest and best **Palm Collection** in the world. Of the more than 2,500 known species of palms, the garden's living collection includes more than 800. This is generally recognized as the world's most important documented palm collection, with more endangered palm species than all of the other botanical gardens in the world combined, according to the World Conservation Monitoring Center. The garden's original palm collection was located primarily in the **Montgomery Palmetum**, but today palms can be found throughout the site.

Palms are mainly tropical or subtropical plants. Not all are trees; some palms grow as shrubs or even as vines climbing into the tree

canopy. The diversity of the various palm species is  truly amazing.
Just consider the following:

- The trunks of palms may grow only several inches or nearly
  200 feet high.
- The diameter of palm trunks varies from 1/4 inch to three feet.
- Palm fronds range from just a few inches to more than thirty
  feet in length.
- Palm seeds may be smaller than the head of a match or weigh
  as much as forty pounds.
- The trunks of palms are most often solitary but may be
  branched, as in the case of the **doum palm** (*Hyphaene thebaica*).

There may be millions, or only a few, specimens of any given
palm species. Some palms still occur in great numbers, one example
being *Copernicia alba,* which grows in solid stands covering hundreds
of square miles in the area where Paraguay, Brazil and Bolivia meet.
(It is estimated that this region alone may contain 500 million
palms.) Some species of palms, however, are severely endangered or
almost extinct. The **bottle palm** (*Hyophorbe lagenicaulis*), a feather-
leaved palm with a swollen trunk, is native to the Mascarene Islands
in the Indian Ocean, where it once covered large areas. Now bottle
palms are nearly extinct in the wild.

Another example of an endangered species is the **Sargent's cherry
palm** (*Pseudophoenix sargentii*). A native of the West Indies, this palm
used to be quite common on Long and Elliot Keys in Florida. In the
early 1900s, it was almost wiped out by collectors of landscaping
plants and through the destruction of native hammocks for pineapple
and lime groves. Seeds collected from Sargent's cherry palms on Long
and Elliot Keys were brought to the Fairchild Tropical Garden; later,
palm seedlings were reintroduced to the Keys.

Several palm species are of great economic importance. For
example, the **coconut palm** (*Cocos nucifera*) is without question the
best known as well as one of the most beautiful palms. A visual icon
of the tropics, the coconut palm has been cultivated for so many
centuries that its origins in the wild are not known. Oblivious to salt
water, the coconut grows in sandy soils along tropical shorelines.
Buoyed by their husks, coconuts are frequently carried by ocean
currents to distant regions, where they will retain their germinating
power for several months after floating in salt water.

To most of us, coconut palms are most familiar as an ornament in garden landscapes, but around the world many people depend on the palm's versatility and usefulness. The meat of the coconut is used for food; when dried it becomes copra, a source of vegetable oil. The hard inner shell of the nut is used to make bottles and cups but also as a fuel or to make charcoal. The husk, called coir, provides fiber used in doormats, etc. Coconut milk is used for cooking or as a beverage. Sap obtained by tapping the flower stalk is a source of sugar, alcohol or vinegar. The trunks of coconut palms yield wood for construction or furniture making. Palm leaves are used for baskets or as roofing material. Hundreds of other uses for every part of the coconut palm could still be mentioned. According to an old Indian saying: "If you take care of a coconut palm for the first seven years of its life, it will take care of you for the rest of your life."

The **date palm** (*Phoenix dactylifera*), native to the Middle East, has been cultivated for fruit since about 6000 B.C. This tree, which requires very little water, starts to bear fruit at five years and may continue bearing fruit for more than a century. One date palm may bear up to 500 pounds of dates each year, which are a major crop of several Middle Eastern countries; it is estimated that Iraq alone has 20 million date palms. Dates have been grown commercially in California since 1890, and today their production in California and Arizona reaches several million pounds a year. The climate of south Florida is, however, not suitable for the production of good-tasting edible dates.

Palms are also important in sugar production. Sugar is produced not only from the **sugar palm** (*Arenga pinnata*) but also from several other species such as the **nipa palm** *(Nypa fruticans)*, the **fishtail palm** (*Caryota urens*), the **talipot palm** (*Corypha umbraculifera*), the **wild date palm** *(Phoenix sylvestris)* and even the **coconut palm** (*Cocos nucifera*). As in the case of the **palmyra palm** (*Borassus flabelifer*), the sap is obtained by tapping the flower stalk. This will start the flow of a few quarts of sap daily, lasting for several weeks.

The oil of the **African oil palm** (*Elaeis guineensis*), native to West Africa, is a valuable commodity and one of the important export products of this region. The worldwide production of oil from African oil palms amounts to millions of tons. The **American oil palm** or **cohune palm** *(Attalea cohune)* and the **scheelea** (*Scheelea zonensis*), both native to Central America, provide oil from their seeds that is used for cooking and in soap manufacture.

The **Seychelles palm** (*Lodoicea maldivica*) produces the largest seed in the world. These endangered palms grow on only three of the islands in the Seychelles, a group of islands in the Indian Ocean. The Seychelles palm is frequently called *coco-de-mer* or "double coconut" after its nut, which resembles two large coconuts joined together. The nuts weigh 30 to 45 pounds, and there may be as many as 60 to 70 such nuts on a single tree. This large fan palm grows about 90 to 100 feet tall. It may flower when it is 20 to 30 years old but does not mature or bear fruit until it reaches at least 100 years old.

Another fascinating palm is the **talipot palm** (*Corypha umbraculifera*), native to India and Sri Lanka. This palm blooms and bears fruit only once in its life, usually when thirty to eighty years old, and then begins to die. The Talipot palm produces the plant kingdom's largest inflorescence, reaching up to 35 feet long, containing as many as 10 million flowers and producing up to a ton of seeds.

**Cycads** are members of an ancient family, descendants of plants known to have existed in the Mesozoic Era from about 225 million to 65 million years ago, the age of dinosaurs. Distributed in tropical and subtropical regions, they represent the oldest living forms of seed-bearing plants.

Cycads are palmlike, woody plants that grow very slowly. The stem, which can be partially or completely buried, contains a large pith surrounded by a fairly narrow zone of soft wood. Cycads are strictly dioecious, meaning that male and female reproductive organs develop on separate plants. Male cones produce pollen, which is then transmitted by the wind to female cones where fertilization occurs.

The Fairchild Tropical Garden has one of the largest and most extensive collections of cycads in the world, with nearly all of the world's 200 known species growing in **Cycad Circle** and throughout the upland area.

In our part of the world, cycads are widely grown as ornamental plants. In other regions, the young leaves and seeds of some species are consumed. Starch obtained from the powdered pith of some cycads is also edible after the toxic alkaloid cycasin is removed, either by thorough washing or by curing the mashed pith in the sun for long periods of time. When ground, this powdery "flour" can be used to prepare bread. **Florida arrowroot** or **coontie** (*Zamia pumila*) is a small cycad with a short underground trunk. Its starchy pith was a major food of Florida's Seminole Indians, who harvested the pith in the winter months when its starch content is highest.

The hot, steamy, and humid environment of the equatorial rain forest is simulated in the **Rain Forest Exhibit**. The high canopy is provided by **live oak trees** (*Quercus virginiana*) and by various tropical trees. A multitude of smaller understory plants, such as huge epiphytic **staghorn ferns** (*Platycerium bifurcatum*), **orchids**, **bromeliads** and **aroids**, grow on the ground and also high in the branches of trees.

Although the rain forest is beautiful, it is also in danger. While enjoying its captivating flora and fauna, we must also work to prevent its further destruction by timber harvesting, agriculture or just "progress" and development. The consequences of these actions are soil erosion, climate changes and a permanent loss of valuable animal and plant species. Can a tropical rain forest regenerate? If it can, how long would it take? Nobody knows the answers. Let's not wait until it's too late.

### The Conservatory

A beautiful, state-of-the-art, 16,400-square-foot **Conservatory** was opened at the garden in the spring of 1996. This exciting structure stands on the site of the old Rare Plant House, which sustained severe damage during Hurricane Andrew in 1992. A grand total of 1,730 species of tropical plants are displayed here.

In addition to displaying rare plants in their natural setting, the Conservatory plays an important role in the garden's conservation efforts. Many of the plants here cannot be grown outdoors in southern Florida. Some of the specimens are too tender to grow in exposed outdoor locations; some are cold-sensitive; others may need more shade, special soil or increased humidity. Any of these conditions can be easily controlled and adjusted in this facility.

The Conservatory provides an educational experience as well. A **Windows to the Tropics** exhibit highlights plant life in tropical environments. The collections are arranged around various themes, such as plant/animal interactions, new plant introductions, plants and people, etc.

Here are just three of the more unusual trees in the garden.

- The **cannonball tree** (*Couroupita guianensis*) is a timber tree native to Guyana. In other tropical countries it is cultivated for its unusual flowers and fruit. The pleasantly fragrant flowers are pollinated by bats in the wild, but in Florida they must be hand-pollinated. The tree's flowers emerge on special floral branches growing from the lower trunk. The fruit of the cannonball tree is four to eight inches in diameter, chocolate brown and quite inedible. The pulp of the fruit is full of seeds and has an unpleasant odor when ripe. It is a sight to see these cannonballs hanging on heavy tendrils suspended from the trunk. On a windy day, the pounding of hard-shelled cannonballs against the trunk and against each other creates quite a noise.

- The **sausage tree** (*Kigelia pinnata*) is indeed an oddity in the plant world. The tree is native to tropical West Africa and is cultivated as a curiosity for its strange, sausage-shaped fruits dangling from its branches. The "sausages" weigh from five to twelve pounds, take a year to ripen and are not edible. However, the Masai people of Africa use the "sausages" to make an alcoholic beverage for use in their festivities and celebrations. The "sausages" are preceded by night blooming, unpleasant smelling, velvety-red flowers that usually open one at a time. In their natural habitat they are pollinated by bats, but in Florida they must be hand-pollinated.

- The **baobab tree** (*Adansonia digitata*), native to Africa, is one of the largest trees in the world. The tree was named after the botanical explorer Michael Adanson, who discovered it in 1794. It is not uncommon for the baobab's barrellike trunk to reach a diameter of 30 feet. Trees with a 100-foot girth are known to exist, although the height of the tree rarely exceeds 60 feet. The baobab quite often looks even fatter than it actually is, because a specimen forty feet tall may have a trunk thirty feet wide. An Arabian legend has it that "the devil plucked up the Baobab, thrust its branches into the ground and left its roots in the air." The age of some of the larger baobabs is estimated at 5,000 years, making it one of the longest-lived species in the world. The baobab tree has adapted to a dry climate marvelously, developing a deep root system, large branches that bear leaves only during the wet season and a pithy trunk with very little wood but great water storage capabilities. A large tree may store several thousands of gallons of water in its fibrous trunk. The baobab tree is also quite useful. The bark's strong fiber is used to make rope and cloth. Furry fruit up to one foot in length hang on long stems and is sought by humans as well as monkeys for its cool and tasty pulp. The leaves are used for leaven or as a vegetable. Quite frequently, a fungus hollows out the trunk of the baobab tree; the trunks are also purposely excavated for use as temporary shelters or as water reservoirs in some parts of Africa. In times of drought elephants often rip open the trunk of the tree to get the water out of its pulp.

The **Moos Memorial Sunken Garden** was created out of a sinkhole. Instead of filling the hole, the Garden's architects created a small oasis of beauty and solitude. Each entrance is guarded by a **live oak** (*Quercus virginiana*). As one descends a gently sloping path carved out of limestone, a waterfall and a small pool suddenly appear. Tall palms tower around the upper walls; **anthuriums, philodendrons, ferns** and **begonias** grow out of rock crevices and lower walls.

The **McLamore Arboretum** displays some 740 species of flowering trees from all tropical regions of the world on 10 acres. No matter when you visit, there is always something in bloom. The **giant shaving brush tree** (*Pseudobombax ellipticum*) offers an explosion of color against a blue sky. The flower buds resemble dark brown, cylindrical acorns a few inches in length. The buds spring open at night; the next morning, petals are curled back to expose long, pink stamens. The flowers look like colorful shaving brushes fastened to the tips of leafless branches. This tree, native to Mexico, is considered one of the world's most beautiful flowering trees.

One of the garden's landmarks, the **flowering vine pergola,** stretches 560 feet along the Old Cutler Road wall. The pergola's stone pillars were constructed out of oolitic limestone by members of the Civilian Conservation Corps just before World War II. A great number of flowering vines provide a beautiful display of colors here throughout the year.

The **Lynn Fort Lummus Endangered Plant Garden** displays several endangered species of Florida and Puerto Rico. Officially, an "endangered" species is one that is getting close to extinction. A "threatened" species could became an endangered one if protective steps are not taken. Once an endangered species becomes extinct, of course, it is lost forever.

The **Gate House Museum of Plant Exploration** exhibits "In Search of Green Treasure," which includes photographs, plant artifacts and real-life experiences of plant explorers traveling the globe to seek out new and unknown plants. The building itself is a historic landmark, built in 1939 and restored in 1995.

The **Lowlands** section of Fairchild Tropical Garden covers fifty-seven acres. These lowlands were marine flats before the bay and the marshes were filled. The creation of lakes here provided additional fill for this area; even more importantly, it created permanent open spaces in accordance with the garden's grand design.

### Mangrove Preserve

The mangrove family, quite common on tropical and subtropical coastlines, includes many species of trees and shrubs. South Florida is an ideal region to study mangroves, since the three main species, **red mangrove** (*Rhizophora mangle*), **black mangrove** (*Avicennia germinans*) and **white mangrove** (*Laguncularia racemosa*), grow in many different local soil types.

Mangroves play an important role in protecting and stabilizing the shoreline. By accumulating in the dense tangle of aerial roots, the decomposing leaves of mangrove stands create new land. The mangroves also help to support a rich marine ecosystem by providing food, nursery grounds and sanctuary for a great variety of marine life, especially for young fishes and shrimp.

Red mangroves are not only salt-water tolerant, they seem to thrive in it, growing along the shoreline and well out into the mudflats. Black mangroves typically grow further inland, covered at high tide but quite exposed during low tide. White mangroves usually grow further away from the water, frequently behind other mangroves. At times all three mangroves may be found growing in mixed stands.

One may not realize that large parts of Fairchild Tropical Garden were originally a mangrove swamp. An original stand of mangroves survives in the Lowlands in their natural state.

### Bahamian Plants

A section of the **Lowlands** was reserved for a collection of rare

Bahamian trees and shrubs, some of which are found only in the Bahamas. Considering the continuing development of the Bahamas, it is possible that some of these plants might become endangered or even extinct.

All of these plants grow quite well in the south Florida climate, which is very similar to that of the Bahamas. Propagated and maintained in the Fairchild Tropical Garden, this collection is readily available for scientific study. Several specimens of the same species are always planted, so that if some are lost in their native island habitat, the species can be reintroduced.

**The Migratory Bird Habitat** is a relatively new addition to the Lowlands. South Florida and the Florida Keys lie along a major flyway for birds migrating to the Caribbean and South America. The canopy trees planted here provide the weary travelers with cover, shelter, and food. Future plantings of additional understory plants will complete this project, allowing it to serve as an extension of the natural feeding areas of the Keys for migratory birds and also as an area where people can see native south Florida trees and plants.

### Chachi House

The newest addition to the Lowlands is a Chachi house, part of the **"People of the Rain Forest"** exhibit. The staff of the Fairchild Tropical Garden wanted to demonstrate what life in a tropical rain forest is like, and the Chachi people warmly embraced the idea.

This exhibit is meant to educate us about the indigenous people of the tropical rain forest in northwestern Ecuador and their surroundings. There are only about 4,000 Chachis left, and the destruction of the rain forest threatens those who remain. The Chachi people are under immense pressure to cut and sell their forest, which provides them with just about everything they need: food, water and shelter. To grasp the tremendous importance of this highly endangered habitat, one must realize that the remaining

tropical rain forests now occupy only a small percentage of the earth's surface yet still account for more than half of the world's plant and animal species.

Three Chachi men came to the garden and built a true replica of a Chachi house from building materials from Ecuador. It is a house on stilts, without walls, constructed from bamboo and palms with a thatched palm roof. The exhibit is complete with dug-out canoes, furnishings and even a garden.

### The Hibiscus Garden

Not to be missed is the Fairchild Tropical Garden hibiscus collection, where one can wander in amazement throughout a multitude of colorful blossoms. The origins of today's hibiscus can be traced to the **Chinese red hibiscus** (*Hibiscus rosa-sinensis*). Today there are several thousand varieties and hybrids of hibiscus. Blooms on most last just one day; hybrids have been developed which usually bloom for two days.

A **Bamboo Garden** was recently established in the Lowlands. Bamboos are grasses, some with woody stems, and may range in height from a few inches to more than 100 feet. Dr. Fairchild was fascinated by the beauty and economic value of bamboo. Many kinds of bamboo are cultivated for their ornamental value, yet very few plants offer more practical uses. The young shoots and seeds of some bamboos are edible. The wood is used for building material; bamboo also goes into furniture, mats and paper.

The Fairchild Tropical garden certainly holds a unique place among the world's leading botanical gardens. A 1992 statement adopted by the Fairchild Tropical Garden Board of Trustees best summarizes the missions and goals of the garden:
- To be a premier tropical botanical garden of the world;
- To set the highest possible standard in landscape design and exhibitions, living collections and horticultural practices;
- To be a primary source of information on tropical plants through research and education;
- To inspire positive attitudes and behavior toward the urban and natural environment.

### Education and Research

Such goals may seem overwhelming; it is certainly no small task to accomplish them. Fortunately, the garden's staff of horticulturists, scientists, curators and educators is actively supported by more than 11,000 garden members and hundreds of dedicated volunteers giving their time, talent, sweat and ideas in order to accomplish the common goal.

The garden's **Montgomery Library** collection of about 8,000 volumes is a remarkable treasure of horticultural and tropical botany books valued by researchers, scientists and students from around the world. The garden's impressive herbarium collection includes more than 80,000 dried plant specimens for research.

The institution plays an extremely important role in the education of grade school pupils and their teachers, the general public, university students and professional botanists. Informal instruction, garden tours, educational workshops and formal seminars are carried out knowledgeably and with enthusiasm. Staff botanists are actively studying rain forests in the West Indies and Central America, learning new ways to classify palms worldwide and describing the effects of fire on Florida's native cycad. They are trying to understand how water flows through the stems of tropical vines and developing better ways to prune and grow tropical fruit trees. The garden's scientists study the life cycles of rare plants of South Florida, advise local governments on the management of natural areas and publish reference books and technical papers about tropical plants. In their search for new specimens, they are also plant explorers, bringing back seeds and cuttings of new plant introductions.

It is projected that twenty percent of the world's biodiversity will be lost in the next twenty-five years, with most of this loss occurring in tropical regions of the world. With this in mind, there is a sense of urgency in collecting and preserving the plants that may one day be the last living specimens of their kind. At the time of this writing, the garden had over 10,000 plants, representing more than 5,000 species, with approximately 7,600 new acquisitions since Hurricane Andrew. The Fairchild Tropical Garden, as a member of the Center for Plant Conservation, has also been designated a national site for endangered species of South Florida, Puerto Rico, and the U.S. Virgin Islands.

We must realize that it is necessary to balance and redefine our relationship with nature, or else many species and endangered ecosystems will be lost forever. Keeping all of the noble goals in mind, let us not lose sight of the most important fact: Fairchild Tropical Garden is a place of enjoyment and great beauty.

# Parrot Jungle and Gardens

*A tropical garden paradise with over 2,000 varieties of plants and 1,000 tropical birds.*

**Address:** 11000 SW 57th Avenue, Miami, FL 33156

**Directions:** Go south on Red Road (SW 57th Avenue) until you see Parrot Jungle on your right side. From U.S. 1, take Killian Drive (SW 112 Street) until you see Parrot Jungle on your left.

**Hours:** 9:30 a.m. to 6:00 p.m. daily

**Admission fee:** yes

**Wheelchair access:** yes

**Facilities:** gift shop, café

**Available:** membership

**Area:** 20 acres

**Phone:** (305) 666-7834; recorded information (305) 669-7035

Without a doubt, Parrot Jungle is a Miami institution and one of the best-known tourist attractions in south Florida. It was the dream of Franz Scherr, who in the Great Depression visualized a tropical jungle with exotic birds, flowers, and trees. To realize his dream, Scherr rented a twenty-acre site, formerly a nudist colony, just off Red Road in South Dade County for $25 a year. On December 20, 1936, the Parrot Jungle and Gardens officially opened to about 100 curious visitors, who paid a 25-cent admission to see 25 parrots and to listen to Franz Scherr describe his small corner of paradise.

Sixty years later, more than 1,000 tropical birds and 2,000 plant varieties are flourishing at

Parrot Jungle. **Tropical Gardens, Cypress Hammock,** or **Canna Lily Garden** await your visit. Paths wind through the jungle under a canopy of tall **cypress** and **palms,** supporting **aroids, orchids,** and **bromeliads** on their trunks and branches. A **Cactus Ravine** displays thriving varieties of cactus from all over the world. Photogenic flamingos flash magnificent colors around **Flamingo Lake,** while parrots display every color imaginable. Take a self-guided tour at your own pace or attend the scheduled shows and presentations.

# Japanese Garden on Watson Island

**Address:** Department of Parks and Recreation, Miami, FL 33133
**Directions:** Heading toward Miami Beach on MacArthur Causeway
  make a left turn to Watson Island.
**Hours:** 8:00 a.m. to 2:00 p.m. daily
**Closed:** holidays
**Admission fee:** no
**Wheelchair access:** yes
**Area:** 1 acre
**Phone:** (305) 579-6944

This small Japanese garden is under the care of the Miami Department of Parks and Recreation. It offers a pleasing combination of plants, rocks, and water: the key ingredients to Japanese garden design.

# The Kampong

*This seven-acre property, the former home of Dr. David Fairchild,*
*includes an astounding collection of rare tropical trees and plants.*

**Address:** 4013 Douglas Road, Coconut Grove, FL 33133
**Directions:** Take U.S. 1 to Douglas Road (SW 37th Avenue). Turn
    south and go about 1 mile to The Kampong entrance.
**Hours:** open the first Sunday of each month
**Admission fee:** yes
**Wheelchair access:** yes
**Available:** group tours by appointment
**Area:** 7 acres
**Phone:** (305) 442-7169

The Kampong is a seven-acre botanical garden located on Biscayne Bay in Coconut Grove, just four miles south of downtown Miami. As part of the National Tropical Botanical Garden, it harbors a rare collection of unusual tropical plants and fruits. Many varieties of palms, flowering trees and ornamental plants thrive here as well.

The Kampong is the former home of Dr. David Fairchild, one of the most distinguished plant collectors, botanists, and horticulturists of his time. As the head of the Seed and Plant Introduction Section of the U.S. Department of Agriculture, Dr. Fairchild was responsible for the introduction of more than 2,000 different species of plants into the United States. Although most of his introductions were tropical fruits, he also brought in many palms, vines, flowering trees, and grains. Many plants commonly grown today as well as food staples were his introductions: polyembryonic mangoes from Indonesia; cotton and dates from Egypt; rice, soybeans, and cherry trees from Japan; wheat from Russia; and cauliflower from Italy—just to mention a few. He planted many specimens either at the USDA's Introduction Station at Chapman Field in Miami or at The Kampong (or at both), often experimenting with plants at The Kampong before taking them to Chapman Field.

Dr. Fairchild surrounded himself with unusual plants that served as reminders of his worldwide travels. The first tree he planted at

The Kampong was a
**kaffir orange**
(*Strychnos nux
vomica*), a Sri Lanka
and Madagascar
native. This
orange has a sweet,
spicy and edible
pulp, but the
seeds are the source
of the poisonous
alkaloid strychnine.
You can see, smell,
and touch hundreds
of other fascinating trees
and plants growing at The
Kampong.

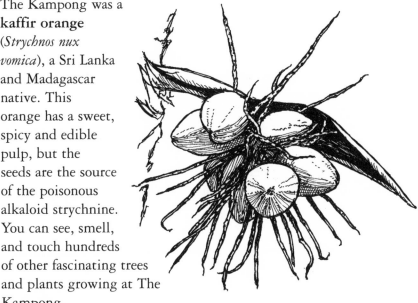

"Kampong" is a Malay word for "village" or "cluster of houses."
The Fairchilds purchased the property in 1916. Many famous people
have visited The Kampong over the years, including Thomas Edison,
Henry Ford and Alexander Graham Bell (Dr. Fairchild's father-in-
law). While at The Kampong, Alexander Graham Bell invented a
method of extracting distilled water from salt water by using solar
energy. This invention, still intact, can be viewed in its original location. After the death of Marion Fairchild, Dr. Fairchild's wife, in
1962, the property was purchased by Catherine Sweeney. In 1984,
the Kampong was entered into the National Register of Historic
Places. Later on, the property became a part of the National Tropical
Botanical Garden.

The mission of The Kampong is probably best summarized in the
September 1989 issue of the "Kampong Notes":

- The main mission is to maintain and augment an aesthetically
  acceptable Garden of labeled tropical plants, both attractive
  and useful, for purposes of education and research, while
  honoring the efforts and interests of its founder, David
  Fairchild.
- The Kampong Garden is open to the public under stated regu-
  lations, including prior application.
- The Kampong Garden collections are documented as far as

possible as to the origin and age, and by voucher specimens, and are supported by an appropriate non-circulating reference library.

- The Kampong Garden encourages research of the plants in its collections and may be able to offer housing to visiting scholars and students.
- The Kampong Garden may offer or sponsor jointly lectures, symposia, or professional meetings, making its facilities available to speakers or small groups.
- The Kampong Garden will publish the "Kampong Notes" and for its pages consider  popular articles relating to its collections and history. Articles based on the research of visiting scientists may be submitted to be considered for the serial publications of the National Tropical Botanical Garden.
- The Kampong Garden maintains an interest in the life, travels, work and contributions of David Fairchild. The Garden will seek to acquire and preserve documentation relating to David Fairchild.

For almost twenty years, The Kampong has also hosted Harvard University Summer School courses and courses for the University of Florida, as well as other colleges and universities. Scholars may take advantage of direct exposure to tropical vegetation without the expensive and at times complicated travel involved with field work. Listed in the National Register of Historic Places.

# John C. Gifford Arboretum of the University of Miami

**Address:** San Amaro Drive and Robbia Avenue, Coral Gables, FL 33124

**Directions:** From U.S. 1 take Red Road (SW 57th Avenue). Turn east on Miller Road (SW 56th Street), then north on San Amaro Drive.

**Hours:** dawn to dusk daily

**Admission fee:** no

**Wheelchair access:** yes

**Area:** 2 acres

**Phone:** (305) 284-5364

The Arboretum was founded in 1947 and named for Dr. John C. Gifford, the first graduate forester in the United States and a professor of tropical forestry at the University of Miami. Over the years, as the Arboretum grew, new trails and plantings were added. In 1950, the Gifford Society of Tropical Botany was formed to promote the study of tropical plants. Today, more than 500 tropical plants thrive here.

# Venetian Pool

**Address:** 2701 DeSoto Boulevard, Coral Gables, FL 33134
**Directions:** From Palmetto Expressway (Hwy. 826) in Miami, take
    exit for SW 24th Street (Coral Way) and go east until Toledo
    Street in Coral Gables. Go south on Toledo Street for 4 blocks.
**Hours:** times may vary, please call
**Admission fee:** yes
**Wheelchair access:** yes
**Facilities:** snack bar
**Area:** 2 acres
**Phone:** (305) 460-5356

George Merrick, the founding father of Coral Gables in 1923, transformed an abandoned, unsightly rock quarry into a spectacular 820,000-gallon Venetian swimming pool fed with cool spring water. A tropical landscape surrounds the pool with **palms, tropical flowers, birds of paradise, coffee plants,** waterfalls, coral caves, and a palm-fringed island. The surrounding buildings are a fine example of Venetian architecture, making the Venetian Pool the most gorgeous place you can imagine to swim. Listed in the National Register of Historic Places.

# Redland Fruit and Spice Park

*The only tropical botanical garden of its kind in the United
States, with 100 varieties of citrus, 65 varieties of bananas, and
40 varieties of grapes. Just come and taste.*

**Address:** 24801 SW 187th Ave., Homestead, FL 33031
**Directions:** From U.S. 1 take 248th Street and go west for 5 miles
to the intersection with SW 187th Avenue (Redland Road). The
park will be on your left.
**Hours:** 10:00 a.m. to 5:00 p.m. daily
**Closed:** New Year's Day, Thanksgiving, Christmas Day
**Admission fee:** yes
**Wheelchair access:** yes
**Facilities:** gift shop
**Available:** classes, workshops, guided tours by appointment
**Area:** 20 acres
**Phone:** (305) 247-5727

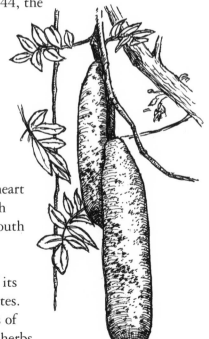

Originally established in 1944, the
Fruit and Spice Park is a
lush twenty-acre tropical
paradise situated in the Redland
area of Dade County. This
fertile area lies in an agricultural
region just thirty miles south of
Miami. The park is owned and
operated by the Metro Dade
County Park and Recreation
Department and is nestled in the heart
of Redland Historic District, which
dates back to the pioneer days of south
Florida.

Its tropical climate makes
Redland the only public garden of its
kind in the continental United States.
It exhibits more than 500 varieties of
fruits, spices, vegetables, nuts and herbs

originating from all around the world. It boasts 40 varieties of **grapes**, 65 varieties of **bananas**, and 100 varieties of **citrus**. The names of other exotic tropical fruit species grown and displayed here is music to the ears of exotic fruit enthusiasts, connoisseurs and growers. Herb and vegetable gardens are also featured, as is a poisonous plant area.

The park takes an important role in educating the public. Formal classes, workshops and botanical tours are conducted on many topics; expert advice can also be obtained on an informal basis. One can obtain gardening advice, such as where to obtain a plant and when to harvest, as well as tips on canning, freezing and cooking. A long list of tropical fruit nurseries and seed sources is also available.

Visitors are allowed to sample the fallen fruit from the ground, although no fruit harvesting from the trees is allowed. To our knowledge, this is the only garden where one can both see and taste tropical exotic fruit. Furthermore, arrangements can be made with the park for collecting seeds and cuttings.

# The Keys

Key West  The Keys

# Audubon House and Tropical Gardens

*A small, mature, period garden of native plants and exotics surrounding an early nineteenth-century home.*

**Address:** 205 Whitehead Street, Key West, FL 33040
**Directions:** From U.S. 1 make right turn onto N. Roosevelt Blvd., which after about 2 miles becomes Truman Avenue. Make right turn on Whitehead Street and travel 6 blocks. The house will be on your right, on the corner of Whitehead and Green Streets.
**Hours:** 9:30 a.m. to 5:00 p.m. daily
**Closed:** Christmas Day
**Admission fee:** yes
**Wheelchair access:** yes
**Facilities:** gift shop
**Area:** 1 acre
**Phone:** (305) 294-2116

In the early 1800s, Key West was a small but bustling town with a remarkably cosmopolitan population. Adventurers and businessmen, refugees and deserters, dreamers and schemers, seamen and wanderers all found their way here. Many of them brought a knowledge of gardening; many tried to recreate the shady or ornamental gardens they had left behind. In addition, ships plying the Caribbean and the oceans of the world quite often brought new plants and trees to be introduced and grown here. But in this period, first and foremost, gardens had to be practical. They had to provide a reliable food supply as well as beauty.

The Audubon House was home to Captain John H. Geiger, a harbor pilot and a master wrecker. The house was built in the early nineteenth century by ship's carpenters and furnished with treasures salvaged from ships wrecked on the reefs of the Florida Keys. Captain Geiger and his heirs occupied this house for more than 120 years. By 1959, however, the property was neglected and in disrepair. In that year, it was purchased by the Wolfson Family Foundation. The decision was made to turn this restored property into a public museum that would recapture the unique culture and spirit of

adventure so fitting to Key West. The museum was named in honor of the 1832 visit to Key West of John James Audubon, who added many of the spectacular water birds he saw to his renowned work *Birds of America.* Walking the streets of Key West today, you may be astounded to find a very similar cast of colorful characters. In the life of Key West, maybe not that much has really changed. Or, as the old saying goes, "The more things change, the more they stay the same."

The gardens surrounding the Audubon House combine native plants as well as ornamental exotics, giving it a unique character and charm. Brick pathways meander under a canopy of tall trees. **Palms** are spread throughout the gardens; **orchids** grow on the trunks and branches of trees everywhere, and their profusion of colors is pleasing. You will find **bromeliads** and **ferns, lilies,** and **irises** wherever you look. Nice specimens of **tropical almond tree** (*Terminalia catappa*) and **sapodilla tree** (*Manilkara zapota*) provide shade. Sapodilla, native to Central America and Mexico, provides deliciously sweet and juicy fruit. Sapodilla trees were also tapped to obtain milky sap, the main source of chicle originally used in the making of chewing gum. A **seven year apple** (*Casasia clusifolia*) has small fruit, more attractive to birds than to people, that hang on the tree for at least a year before they ripen. (Audubon used this tree, which is native to the Florida Keys, as a background for his painting of the mangrove cuckoo.) The **geiger tree** (*Cordia sebestena*) is a threatened species that is native to the Florida Keys and West Indian Islands. It has rough leaves and geranium-like orange blossoms and is quite salt-tolerant, therefore recommended for seaside plantings. Its common name was bestowed by Audubon in honor of Captain Geiger. During his 1832 Keys visit, Audubon painted the white-crowned pigeon sitting on the branch of a blossoming geiger tree.

*Worth Seeing:* Audubon House is the meticulously restored home of Captain John Huling Geiger. The house is furnished with authentic pieces typical of nineteenth-century Key West as well as original engravings by John James Audubon.

# Key West Botanical Garden

**Address:** P.O. Box 2436, Key West, FL 33045
**Directions:** Going south on U.S. 1, make a right turn on College
    Road on Stock Island just before Cow Key bridge (MM 5);
    proceed 1.5 miles to the garden.
**Hours:** sunrise to sunset daily
**Admission fee:** no
**Wheelchair access:** yes
**Facilities:** none
**Area:** 11 acres
**Phone:** (305) 296-6606

The garden was started in 1934 under the Federal Emergency Relief Administration. From the initial six acres, it gradually expanded to fifty acres. In addition to native trees, many exotic tropical species were planted here. During and after World War II, the garden suffered from a period of neglect; some areas were converted to other uses. In 1961, with only eleven acres remaining, it was designated by the city of Key West as a botanical garden and arboretum as well as a permanent wildlife sanctuary. The garden was restored and for close to twenty years was maintained by the Key West Garden Club.

In 1988, the Key West Botanical Garden Society was formed, and in 1991 the society assumed the management of the Garden. It is their mission "to develop, preserve, and maintain the Key West Botanical Garden as a botanical garden, arboretum, and wildlife refuge and to encourage educational use for the visitors and residents of Key West." Along the trails, blue labels represent the native plants and green labels represent the exotic ones (a trail map is available at the garden entrance). The garden provides a habitat for butterflies, as well as resident and migratory birds.

# Ernest Hemingway Home and Museum

**Address:** 907 Whitehead Street, Key West, FL 33040

**Directions:** From U.S. 1 make right turn onto N. Roosevelt Blvd., which after about 2 miles becomes Truman Avenue. Make right turn onto Whitehead Street and travel for 1 block. The house will be on your right.

**Hours:** 9:00 a.m. to 5:00 p.m. daily.

**Admission fee:** yes

**Wheelchair access:** partial

**Facilities:** gift shop

**Area:** 1 acre

**Phone:** (305) 294-1575

The home of the famous writer was built of native rock in Spanish Colonial style. Here Hemingway wrote several of his most important works. The home in which he lived from 1931 to 1961 is furnished with items the author collected during his world travels. It is set in a mature, lush tropical garden that features many exotic species from all over the world. The house has been designated a National Historic Landmark.

# Nancy Forrester's Secret Garden

**Address:** 1 Free School Lane, Key West, FL 33040

**Directions:** From U.S. 1 make right turn onto N. Roosevelt Blvd., which after about 2 miles becomes Truman Avenue. Make right turn onto Simonton Street and travel 4 blocks. The garden is located at the end of Free School Lane, which is between Southard and Fleming Streets.

**Hours:** 10:00 a.m. to 5:00 p.m. daily

**Admission fee:** yes

**Wheelchair access:** yes

**Facilities:** art gallery

**Area:** 1 acre

**Phone:** (305) 294-0015

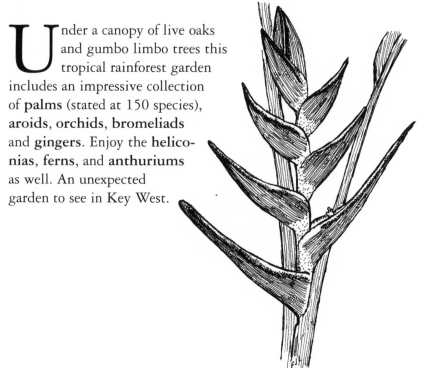

Under a canopy of live oaks and gumbo limbo trees this tropical rainforest garden includes an impressive collection of **palms** (stated at 150 species), **aroids, orchids, bromeliads** and **gingers**. Enjoy the **helico-nias, ferns,** and **anthuriums** as well. An unexpected garden to see in Key West.

# Little White House Museum

**Address:** 111 Front Street, Key West, FL 33040

**Directions:** From U.S. 1 make right turn onto N. Roosevelt Blvd., which after about 2 miles becomes Truman Avenue. Make right turn on Whitehead Street and travel 4 blocks, then turn left on Southard Street. After 2 blocks make right turn on Front Street. The house will be on your right.

**Hours:** 9:00 a.m. to 5:00 p.m. daily

**Admission fee:** yes

**Wheelchair access:** yes

**Facilities:** gift shop

**Area:** 1 acre

**Phone:** (305) 294-9911

Inside of Truman Annex is the house that served as a vacation retreat for presidents Harry S. Truman, Dwight Eisenhower, and John F. Kennedy. The house has been restored to its 1948 appearance. After visiting the Little White House, explore the surrounding grounds. A brochure is available to help you to identify the trees and plants on your self-guided botanical tour. Listed in the National Register of Historic Places.

# West Martello Tower and Garden Center

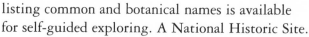

**Address:** P.O. Box 2277, Key West, FL 33045

**Directions:** Follow Roosevelt Blvd. (SR A1A) to the south side of the island. The tower is next to county beach at Atlantic Boulevard and White Street.

**Hours:** 9:30 a.m. to 3:15 p.m. Tuesday to Saturday

**Closed:** Sunday and Monday

**Admission fee:** donation

**Wheelchair access:** yes

**Facilities:** no

**Area:** 1 1/2 acres

**Phone:** (305) 294-3210

The West Martello Tower, a Civil War fort, is now home to the Key West Garden Club. What once were the parade grounds of the fort is now a lush tropical garden with an impressive collection of native and exotic plants, **orchids**, and **bromeliads**. All the plants are labeled; a nice brochure listing common and botanical names is available for self-guided exploring. A National Historic Site.

# Other Places of Interest to Garden and Plant Lovers

## Northwest

### Blackwater River State Park
Route 1, Box 57-C
Holt, FL 32564
(850) 983-5363
Nature trails through diverse plant communities along Blackwater River, considered one of the purest sand-bottom rivers in the world.

### St. Marks National Wildlife Refuge
1255 Lighthouse Road
P.O. Box 68
St. Marks, FL 32355
(850) 925-6121
Almost 70,000 acres, with 40 percent uplands and 60 percent wetlands. Several major habitats, many endangered and threatened species, and environmental education.

### Torreya State Park
Route 2, Box 70
Bristol, FL 32321
(850) 643-2674
Rare Torreya trees grow only in this region along the Apalachiocala River bluffs.

### Wakulla Springs State Park
1 Spring Drive
Wakulla Springs, FL 32305
(850) 922-3632
Some Florida Champion trees are here, located in upland hardwood hammock. One of the world's deepest and largest freshwater springs.

# Northeast

## Devil's Millhopper State Geological Site
4732 Millhopper Road
Gainesville, FL 32606
(352) 955-2008
A huge, 120-foot deep sinkhole with diverse plant life.

## Marjory K. Rawlings State Historic Site
Route 3, Box 92
Hawthorne, FL 32640
(352) 466-3672
The author's home, fruit garden, and citrus grove.

## Paynes Prairie State Preserve
Route 2, Box 41
Micanopy, FL 32667
(352) 466-3397
Twenty distinct biological communities are represented here.

# Central

### Archbold Biological Station
Rt.2  Box 180
Lake Placid, FL 33852
(941) 465-2571
Self-guiding labeled nature trail, numbered interpretive stations.

### Dickson Azalea Garden
Rosegarden Drive
Orlando, FL 32803
(407) 246-2287
In a city park, a trail meanders alongside a creek banked with azaleas and ferns.

### Environmental Learning Center
255 Live Oak Drive
Vero Beach, FL 32963
(561) 589-5050
Nature trails, native plant garden, exhibits in the Nature Center.

### Highlands Hammock State Park
5931 Hammock Road
Sebring, FL 33872
(941) 386-6094
Several nature trails (some with interpretive signs), boardwalk, and an interpretive center explaining the park's plant communities and wildlife. Enormous live oaks, some believed to be 1,000 years old, stands of hardwoods, wild orange trees, cypress, ferns, and the largest sabal palm in Florida.

### Mead Garden
1300 South Denning Drive
Winter Park, FL 32789
(407) 623-3275
City park, boardwalk, nature trails, butterfly garden.

### Rock Springs Run State Preserve
c/o Wekiwa Springs State Park
1800 Wekiwa Circle
Apopka, FL 32712
(407) 884-2009
This preserve is 8,750 acres, with a variety of plant communities such as pine flatwoods, sand pine scrub, bayheads, hammocks, and swamps.

### The Street Audubon Nature Center
115 Lameraux Road
Winter Haven, FL 33884
(941) 324-7304
A 42-acre formal Street estate. Nature trails and natural history programs; gardens being restored.

### Walt Disney World Resort
P.O. Box 10,000
Lake Buena Vista
Orlando, FL 32830
(407) 824-4321
Theme gardens with spectacular horticultural displays.

# Central East

## Bulow Creek State Park
3351 Old Dixie Highway
Ormond Beach, FL 32174
(904) 676-4040
Nature trail and an 800-year-old Fairchild live oak.

## Tomoka State Park
2099 North Beach Street
Ormond Beach, FL 32174
(904) 676-4050
Nature trail, scenic oaks.

# Central West

### Busch Gardens
3000 Tampa Blvd.
Tampa, FL 33612
(813) 971-5082
Amusement park with an African theme, as well as a conservation-focused zoo. Some beautiful horticultural displays, an Orchid Canyon, and Bird Gardens.

### DeSoto National Memorial
P.O. Box 15390
Bradenton, FL 34280
(941) 792-0458
A half-mile nature trail passes mangrove, epiphytes, cacti, yucca, and massive gumbo limbo trees. Museum in the visitor center.

### Gizella Kopsick Palm Arboretum
North Shore Drive
St. Petersburg, FL 33701
(813) 893-7335
Parklike setting covering 2 acres; 200 palms representing 45 species, cycads.

### Hillsborough River State Park
15402 U.S 301 North
Thonotosassa, FL 33591
(813) 987-6771
Eight miles of nature trails through hammocks of sabal palms, live oaks, magnolias, and hickories.

### Lowry Park Zoo
7530 North Blvd.
Tampa, FL 33604
(813) 932-0245
Nice horticultural displays, azaleas, bromeliads.

## *Myakka River State Park*
13207 SR 72
Sarasota, FL 33241
(941) 361-6511
Interpretive center, nature trails with interpretive markers, live oaks, and sabal palm hammocks.

## *Pinellas Botanical Learning Center*
12175 125th Street
Largo, FL 33540
(813) 582-2110
Parklike setting, pineland nature trails.

# Southwest

### Big Cypress National Preserve
HCR 61, Box 110
Ochopee, FL 33943
(941) 695-4111
Nature trails, scenic loop drive, interpretive center. The few remaining giant bald cypress are 600 to 700 years old.

### Briggs Nature Center
401 Shell Island Road
Naples, FL 34113
(941) 775-8569
Self-guiding trail, boardwalk through pinelands, scrub oak, salt marsh, and mangroves. Nature displays.

### Calusa Nature Center & Planetarium
3450 Ortiz Avenue
Naples, FL 33905
(941) 275-3435
Boardwalk and nature trails, museum, Audubon aviary.

### Charlotte Harbor Environmental Center
10941 Burnt Store Road
Punta Gorda, FL 33955
(941) 575-4800
Nature trails through pine and palmetto flatwoods. Plants are identified along the trail.

### Collier–Seminole State Park
20200 E. Tamiami Trail
Naples, FL 33961
(941) 394-3397
A tropical hammock trail and a 6.5-mile nature trail. The rare Florida royal palm is common here; many threatened or endangered animal species.

### Corkscrew Swamp Sanctuary
375 Sanctuary Road
Naples, FL 33964
(941) 657-3771
Two-mile boardwalk with detailed information on plants and
plant communities. The virgin stands of ancient bald cypress are
said to be the largest in the country. Some trees are 500 years old
and stand 130 feet tall with a girth of more than 25 feet.

### Everglades Wonder Gardens
270180 Old U.S. 1
Bonita Springs, FL 33959
Zoo with large display of Florida wildlife, exotic birds in lush
botanical garden setting.

### Fakahatchee Strand State Preserve
P.O. Box 548
Copeland, FL 33926
(941) 695-4593
Forests of bald cypress, and Florida's largest stand of native royal
palms, sabal palms, laurel oaks, and red maples. The largest
concentration and variety of epiphytic orchids in North America,
as well as bromeliads, ferns, and many species of rare plants.

### J. N. "Ding" Darling National Wildlife Refuge
1 Wildlife Drive
Sanibel, FL 33957
(941) 472-1100
Nature trails, boardwalk through tropical hammock, many West
Indian plant species. A sanctuary for resident and migratory
birds and a birder's paradise.

### Koreshan State Historic Site
P.O. Box 7
Estero, FL 33928
(941) 992-0311
Remains of Koreshan utopian settlement, remnants of gardens,
nature trail.

### Matanzas Pass Preserve
Oaks Street
Ft. Myers Beach, FL 33931
(941) 338-3300
Unspoiled live-oak hammock and mangrove swamp on Estero
Bay. Native trees, palms, trails, and boardwalks.

### Naples Nature Center—The Conservancy
1450 Merrihue Drive
Naples, FL 34102
(941) 262-0304
Nature trails with interpretive signs, boardwalk, natural history
museum, aviary.

### Sanibel–Captiva Conservation Foundation
3333 Sanibel(Captiva Road
Sanibel, FL 33957
(941) 472-2329
Nature trails, native plant nursery, interpretive displays.

### Six Miles Cypress Slough Preserve
Six Mile Cypress Pkwy.
Ft. Myers, FL 33908
(941) 432-2004
A 1 1/2-mile boardwalk trail allowing you to observe several
distinct slough plant communities in this wetland ecosystem.
Pond cypress, mixed hardwoods, native plants, ferns, orchids.

# Southeast

### Arthur R. Marshall Loxahatchee National Wildlife Refuge
10216 Lee Road
Boynton Beach, FL 33437
(561) 732-3684
Interpretive center, nature trails, cypress swamp boardwalk, bald cypress, ferns, epiphytes.

### Blowing Rocks Preserve
574 South Beach Road
Hobe Sound, FL 33455
(561) 744-6668
Trails through native habitats (oceanfront dune, coastal strand, mangrove wetlands, and tropical hardwood hammock). Butterfly garden. Blowing rocks (at high tide the sea breaking against the rocks sprays seawater up to 50 feet skyward). Spectacular.

### "Doc" Thomas House and Environmental Center
5530 Sunset Drive
South Miami, FL 33143
(305) 666-5111
Pineland gardens, Moreton Bay figs, palms, native plants at the headquarters of the Tropical Audubon Society.

### Everglades National Park
40001 State Road 9336
Homestead, FL 33034
(305) 242-7700
This park is 1.5 million acres and has a multitude of unique plants and plant communities, as well as many different ways to see them.

### Fern Forest Nature Center
201 Lyons Road South
Pompano Beach, FL 33068
(954) 970-0150
Nature trails, boardwalk, native trees and plants, many fern species.

## Garden of Our Lord
Saint James Evangelical Lutheran Church
110 Phoenetia Avenue
Coral Gables, FL 33134
(305) 443-0014
Small garden, adjacent to the church, planted with trees and
plants mentioned in the Bible.

## Gumbo Limbo Environmental Complex
1801 N. Ocean Blvd.
Boca Raton, FL 33432
(561) 338-1473
Includes a self-guiding coastal hammock boardwalk trail with
plants identified; interpretive displays.

## Hobe Sound National Wildlife Refuge
13620 SE Federal Hwy.
Hobe Sound, FL 33455
(561) 546-2067
Coastal sand dunes, mangrove forest, self-guiding trail, interpretive center.

## John D. MacArthur Beach State Park
10900 SR 703 (A1A)
North Palm Beach, FL 33408
(561) 624-6950
A mixture of coastal and tropical hammock and mangroves.
Nature trails. Many native, rare, or endangered plants.

## Jonathan Dickinson State Park
16450 SE Federal Hwy.
Hobe Sound, FL 33455
(561) 546-2771
Nature trails through slash pine woodlands and cypress swamp.
Observation tower on top of 86-foot high "mountain," one of the
highest natural points in south Florida.

### Merrick House
907 Coral Way
Coral Gables, FL 33134
(305) 460-5361
A garden surrounding the historic house of Reverend Solomon
G. Merrick, whose son George became a founding father of Coral
Gables. The house is listed in the National Register of Historic
Places. Gardens feature magnificent, mainly pre-1920s fruit
trees: avocados, wild guavas, large citrus trees, and lychees.

### Miami Beach Garden Center and Conservatory
2000 Convention Center Drive
Miami Beach, FL 33139
(305) 673-7720
Display gardens, orchids, bromeliads.

### Miami Metro Zoo
12400 SW 152nd Street
Miami, FL 33177
(305) 251-0400
Many horticultural displays, palms, orchids.

### Monkey Jungle
14805 SW 216th Street
Miami, FL 33170
(305) 235-1611
Wildlife park displaying monkeys. Re-creation of Amazonian
rain forest, many native species of plants.

### Pine Jog Environmental Center
16301 Summit Blvd.
West Palm Beach, FL 33404
(561) 686-6600
Nature trails through live oak/sabal palm hammock, pine flatwoods, and sawgrass marsh.

### Secret Woods Nature Center
2701 West SR 84
Ft. Lauderdale, FL 33312
(954) 791-1030
Interpretive center, self-guiding nature trails, trail booklet.

### St. Lucie Inlet State Preserve
c/o Jonathan Dickinson State Park
16450 SE Federal Hwy.
Hobe Sound, FL 33455
(561) 546-2771
Atlantic Ocean barrier island accessible by private watercraft only.
A 3,300-foot boardwalk through mangrove forests and coastal
hammocks. Cabbage palms, live oaks, wild limes, paradise trees,
ferns.

### Stranahan House
335 SE 6th Avenue
Ft. Lauderdale, FL 33301
(954) 524-4736
Small garden surrounding this historic home on New River.

# The Keys

### Bahia Honda State Park
36850 Overseas Hwy.
Big Pine Key, FL 33043
(305) 872-2353
Several biological plant communities, including tropical hardwood hammock, mangrove forest, coastal berm, and beach dune. Many plants of Caribbean origin as well as rare and unusual plants: silver palm, key thatch palm, yellow satinwood, manchineel. One of the largest remaining stands of the threatened silver palms in the United States. Specimens of yellow satinwood and silver palm have been certified as national Champion trees.

### John Pennekamp Coral Reef State Park
P.O. Box 487
Key Largo, FL 33037
(305) 451-1202
Many rare and endangered plants can be seen here.

### Lignumvitae Key State Botanical Site
P.O. Box 1052
Islamorada, FL 33036
(305) 664-4815
Guided walks along nature trails winding through the virgin tropical forest. Many species of native plants and trees.

### Museums at Crane's Point
5550 Overseas Highway
Marathon, FL 33050
(305) 743-9100
Nature trails, interpretive palm hammock trails, native plants and trees. Florida Keys history.

# Where to See Specific Types of Flora

*Note:* This listing only includes gardens with major displays.

**Agaves:**                Fairchild Tropical Garden

**Azaleas:**               Ravine State Gardens
                           Eden State Gardens
                           Washington Oaks State Gardens
                           Maclay State Gardens
                           Bok Tower Gardens

**Bamboos:**               Kanapaha Botanical Gardens
                           Fairchild Tropical Gardens
                           Marie Selby Botanical Gardens
                           Edison Winter Home

**Bananas:**               Redland Fruit and Spice Park
                           Fairchild Tropical Garden
                           Flamingo Gardens
                           ECHO Gardens
                           Marie Selby Botanical Gardens

**Banyan Trees:**          Edison Winter Home
                           Marie Selby Botanical Gardens
                           Cypress Gardens

**Baobab Trees:**          Fairchild Tropical Garden

**Bromeliads:**            Marie Selby Botanical Gardens
                           Fairchild Tropical Garden
                           Flamingo Gardens

| | |
|---|---|
| Cacti & Succulents: | Fairchild Tropical Garden |
| | Parrot Jungle |
| | Marie Selby Botanical Gardens |
| | Harry P. Leu Gardens |
| Camellias: | Harry P. Leu Gardens |
| | Kanapaha Botanical Gardens |
| | Maclay State Gardens |
| | Bok Tower Gardens |
| Cannonball Trees: | Fairchild Tropical Garden |
| Carnivorous Plants: | University of South Florida Botanical Garden |
| | Kanapaha Botanical Garden |
| Chinese Gardens: | Society of the Four Arts Botanical and Sculpture Gardens |
| Cycads: | Fairchild Tropical Garden |
| | Edison Winter Home |
| | Marie Selby Botanical Gardens |
| Ferns: | Fairchild Tropical Garden |
| | Marie Selby Botanical Gardens |
| Flowering Trees: | Fairchild Tropical Garden |
| | Flamingo Gardens |
| | Maclay State Gardens |
| Gingers: | Fairchild Tropical Garden |
| | Flamingo Gardens |
| | Harry P. Leu Gardens |
| Heliconias: | Fairchild Tropical Garden |
| | Flamingo Gardens |
| Herb Gardens: | Kanapaha Botanical Gardens |
| | University of South Florida Botanical Garden |
| | Cypress Gardens |

| | |
|---|---|
| **Hibiscus:** | Fairchild Tropical Garden<br>Marie Selby Botanical Gardens<br>Flamingo Gardens<br>Harry P. Leu Gardens |
| **Japanese Gardens:** | Morikami Museum and Japanese<br>    Gardens<br>Japanese Garden at Watson Island<br>Heathcote Botanical Gardens |
| **Magnolias:** | Washington Oaks State Gardens<br>Bok Tower Gardens<br>Maclay State Gardens |
| **Orchids:** | Marie Selby Botanical Gardens<br>Fairchild Tropical Garden<br>World of Orchids |
| **Palms:** | Fairchild Tropical Garden<br>Harry P. Leu Gardens<br>Kanapaha Botanical Gardens<br>Edison Winter Home<br>Ann Norton Sculpture Gardens<br>Nancy Forrester's Secret Garden |
| **Panama Candle Trees:** | Flamingo Gardens<br>Redland Fruit and Spice Park<br>Fairchild Tropical Garden |
| **Rainbow Bark Eucalyptus:** | Fairchild Tropical Garden<br>Mounts Botanical Garden |
| **Rose Gardens:** | Harry P. Leu Gardens<br>Ringling Museums<br>Washington Oaks State Gardens<br>Butterfly World |

**Sausage Trees:**          Fairchild Tropical Garden
                            Edison Winter Home
                            Redland Fruit and Spice Park
                            Parrot Jungle and Gardens
                            Society of the Four Arts Botanical and
                                Sculpture Gardens

**Tropical Fruit:**         Redland Fruit and Spice Park
                            The Kampong
                            ECHO
                            Marie Selby Botanical Gardens

**Vines:**                  Fairchild Tropical Garden
                            Butterfly World
                            Kanapaha Botanical Gardens

**Water Lilies:**           Slocum Water Gardens
                            Kanapaha Botanical Gardens

# A Calendar of Florida Garden Events

## January

**Camellia Show**
Harry P. Leu Gardens
(407) 246-2620

**Redland Natural Arts Festival**
Redland Fruit and Spice Park
(305) 247-5727

**Poinsettia Festival**
Cypress Gardens
(941) 324-2111

## February

**Orchid Show and Sale**
Fairchild Tropical Garden
(305) 667-1651

**Rose Show and Sale**
Fairchild Tropical Garden
(305) 667-1651

**Winter Plant Sale**
Mounts Botanical Garden
(561) 233-1749

# March

### Spring Plant Show and Sale
Flamingo Gardens
(954) 473-2955

### Bromeliad Show and Sale
Fairchild Tropical Garden
(305) 667-1651

### Palm Show and Sale
Fairchild Tropical Garden
(305) 667-1651

### Spring Plant Sale
Marie Selby Botanical Gardens
(941) 366-5731

### Bonsai Society Show
Marie Selby Botanical Gardens
(941) 366-5731

### Plant Sale
Harry P. Leu Gardens
(407) 246-2620

### Azalea Festival
Ravine State Gardens
(904) 329-3721

### Heritage Day at Maclay
Maclay State Gardens
(850) 487-4556

### Spring Flower Festival
Cypress Gardens
(941) 324-2111

# April

### Orchid Show and Sale
Flamingo Gardens
(954) 473-2955

### Bougainvillea Show and Sale
Fairchild Tropical Garden
(305) 667-1651

### Rain Forest Festival
Fairchild Tropical Garden
(305) 667-1651

### Bromeliad Society Show
Marie Selby Botanical Gardens
(941) 366-5731

### Spring Plant Sale
Mounts Botanical Garden
(561) 233-1749

### University of South Florida Botanical Garden
Spring Plant Festival
(813) 974-2329

### Spring Flower Festival
Cypress Gardens
(941) 324-2111

# May

### Spring Palm and Cycad Sale
Flamingo Gardens
(954) 473-2955

*Begonia Show and Sale*
Fairchild Tropical Garden
(305) 667-1651

*Tropical Flowering Tree Show and Sale*
Fairchild Tropical Garden
(305) 667-1651

*Cactus and Succulent Show and Sale*
Fairchild Tropical Garden
(305) 667-1651

*Bonsai Show and Sale*
Fairchild Tropical Garden
(305) 667-1651

*Redland International Orchid Show*
Redland Fruit and Spice Park
(305) 247-5727

*Spring Flower Festival*
Cypress Gardens
(941) 324-2111

# June

*Bamboo Show and Sale*
Fairchild Tropical Garden
(305) 667-1651

*Fern Show and Sale*
Fairchild Tropical Garden
(305) 667-1651

*Tropical Fruit Festival*
Mounts Botanical Garden
(561) 233-1749

*Victorian Garden Party*
Cypress Gardens
(941) 324-2111

# July

*July is Mango Month! International Mango Festival*
Fairchild Tropical Garden
(305) 667-1651

*Summer Plant Fair*
Marie Selby Botanical Gardens
(941) 366-5731

*Tropical Agricultural Fiesta*
Redland Fruit and Spice Park
(305) 247-5727

*Garden Sale*
Heathcote Botanical Garden
(561) 464-4672

*Victorian Garden Party*
Cypress Gardens
(941) 324-2111

# August

*Victorian Garden Party*
Cypress Gardens
(941) 324-2111

# September

*Fall Palm and Cycad Sale*
Flamingo Gardens
(954) 473-2955

### Aroid Show and Sale
Fairchild Tropical Garden
(305) 667-1651
### Gesneriad Show and Sale
Fairchild Tropical Garden
(305) 667-1651

## October

### Heliconia Show and Sale
Fairchild Tropical Garden
(305) 667-1651

### Hibiscus Show and Sale
Fairchild Tropical Garden
(305) 667-1651

### Members Day Sale
Fairchild Tropical Garden
(305) 667-1651

### Fall Plant Festival
University of South Florida Botanical Garden
(813) 974-2329

## November

### Palm Show and Sale
Fairchild Tropical Garden
(305) 667-1651

### Ramble
Fairchild Tropical Garden
(305) 667-1651

### Mum Festival
Cypress Gardens
(941) 324-2111

### Fall Plant Fair
Marie Selby Botanical Gardens
(941) 366-5731

### Fall Plant Sale
Mounts Botanical Garden
(561) 233-1749

### Poinsettia Festival
Cypress Gardens
(941) 324-2111

### Garden Festival
Heathcote Botanical Gardens
(561) 464-4672

# December

### Leu Holidays
Harry P. Leu Gardens
(407) 246-2620

# Index

Page numbers in **bold** indicate photographs.

# H

Hammock
coastal, 158, 160
cypress, 126
live oak, 37, 156, 159
native, 106
palm, 31
subtropical hardwood, 106
tropical, 155, 158, 161
Hammock Trail, 111
Harry P. Leu Gardens, 38–40
Hearst, William Randolph,
108–109
Heathcote Botanical Gardens,
61–62
Heather, 94
Hedychium
coccineum, 39
coronarium, 39, 54
gardneranum, 66
Heliconia, 41, 66, 104, 106,
142
Hemingway, Ernest, 141
Herb garden, 31, 40, 62, 66,
96, 134
Herbs, 66, 87, 133
Hercules club tree, 66
Heron, 107
Hibiscus, 40, 72, 106
Collection, 40
Garden, 72, 106, 122
rosa-sinensis, 122
Hickory, 51, 152
Highlands Hammock State
Park, 149
Hillsborough River State Park,
152

Historic Spanish Point, Osprey,
16, 79
Historic Wray Home, 106
Hobe Sound National Wildlife
Refuge, 158
Hoffman, F. Burrall, 110
Holly Collection, 56
Hume, Dr. H. Harold, 25
Hummingbird garden, 31, 106
Hura crepitans, 105
Hyophorbe lagenicaulis, 70,
114
Hyphaene thebaica, 114

# I

Ibis, 107
Ice Skating Shows, 43
Illicium floridanum, 16
Interpretive
center, 153–154,
157–158, 160
signs, 149, 154–156, 158,
161
Ipe tree, 66
Iris Garden, 106
Irises, 17, 56, 138
Iron Mountain, 45
Italian Garden, 25
Ivy Lane, 56
Ivy, 56

# J

J. N. "Ding" Darling National
Wildlife Refuge, 155
Japanese Garden on Watson
Island, 127